DARK HORSE

"A dark horse, which had never been thought of,
and which the careless St. James had never even observed
in the list, rushed past the grandstand
in sweeping triumph."

THE YOUNG DUKE, BENJAMIN DISRAELI,
EARL OF BEACONSFIELD

"In no other department of human knowledge
has there been such a universal and persistent habit
of misrepresenting the truth of history
as in matters relating to the horse."

THE HORSE IN AMERICA, JOHN H. WALLACE

DARK HORSE

Unraveling the mystery of Nearctic

MURIEL ANNE LENNOX

Beach House Books
Toronto

Beach House Books
25 Leuty Avenue, Toronto, Canada M4E 2R2

National Library of Canada Cataloguing in Publication Data
Lennox, Muriel, 1942-
Dark Horse: unravelling the mystery of Nearctic
Includes bibliographical references
ISBN 0-9699025-2-2
1. Nearctic (Race horse) 2. Race horses—Canada—Biography.
1. Title

SF355.N42L45 2001   798.4'0092'9   C2001-903249-8

Editor: Charis Wahl
Design: Saskia Rowley

First edition

Printed in Canada by Quebecor Printing Inc.

CONTENTS

"So Pete, tell us about Nearctic. What was he like?"

Gordon (Pete) McCann, the legendary trainer of the horses of Windfields Farm, inhaled deeply, looked up at the ceiling, and sighed.

The room, overflowing with Pete's children, grandchildren, and great-grandchildren, had fallen silent in anticipation of his response. It was the summer of 1999, a gathering of the McCann family, and its ninety-one year old patriarch sat stoically in one corner—the centre of everyone's attention.

Pete sighed several more times, his eyes and attention still focused on the ceiling—as if he had lapsed into memory and was pondering how to give form to the ensuing story. No one in the room spoke, nor moved. Even the youngsters seemed mesmerized by the drama, the suspense.

Pete McCann was a brilliant, gifted horseman—some, like champion jockey Ron Turcotte, claim Pete was the greatest Thoroughbred trainer in history. Pete would not agree; he was extremely modest, almost painfully shy. He was also a man of few words, so the prospect of hearing him reminisce was considered a rare and cherished event. Furthermore, it was part of the McCann family lore that Pete had had a very special relationship with Nearctic.

After what seemed like an eternity, Pete scanned the panorama of eager faces, appeared ready to speak, but in a moment, sighed once again, shook his head, and said nothing. He smiled kindly; subject closed.

Throughout the afternoon, Pete talked about other horses he trained—Bunty Lawless, Canadiana, New Providence, Viceregal. But every time the conversation turned to Nearctic, he deftly changed the topic.

Beginning in 1950, for twenty years, Pete McCann conditioned all the great Windfields horses; he started Northern Dancer and Victoria Park and Vice Regent and Flaming Page; he trained Canada's first two Triple Crown winners, New Providence and Canebora; six Queen's Plate winners; and eight Canadian Horses of the Year.

But none of all those hundreds of horses in his care has had a greater influence on the Thoroughbred breed than Nearctic—the one horse he refused to discuss.

The seeds that grew into *Dark Horse* took root when I was presented with two distinct challenges: a young horse and an old mystery. They entered my life almost in tandem. Initially I thought both assignments would be reasonably straightforward. I was wrong.

The young horse, a beautiful Thoroughbred gelding, proved extremely difficult to handle. Both his groom and I were, on separate occasions, badly injured by him. The old mystery did not unfold much more smoothly; but somewhere along the line I came to suspect that horse and the mystery were interconnected.

The horse is Val d'Argent. His dam is French Influence, a granddaughter of Nearctic; his sire, Silver Deputy, a great-great-grandson of Nearctic.

Early on, I saw Val d'Argent in terms of his relationship to Northern Dancer, inspiration of my passion for Thoroughbreds and Thoroughbred horse racing. I knew little of his sire, Nearctic. I was a child when Nearctic raced, and in 1968 he was syndicated and exiled to Maryland to stand at Mrs. du Pont's Woodstock Farm.

Val d' Argent, other than his volatility, bears little resemblance to Northern Dancer. Tall, elegant, and very well balanced, Val d' Argent looks more like the Nijinsky side of the family. By coincidence, when Val d' Argent entered my life, I was writing about Nijinsky in my weekly series on the world's great Thoroughbreds for the Japanese magazine, *Gallop*. It was my research for the story of Nijinsky that compelled me to follow the trail that resulted in *Dark Horse*.

I loved Nijinsky. I was captivated by his extraordinary presence.

I was at the yearling sale, when George Scott bought the colt for Charles Engelhard. I followed Nijinsky's racing career more closely than I followed the Beatles, and not long before Nijinsky died, I made a pilgrimage to Kentucky to spend an afternoon simply sitting under a tree outside his paddock watching this great champion graze.

Nijinsky was the supreme achievement of Windfields Farm. But Nijinsky didn't just happen. Nandi, the pivotal foundation broodmare in the Windfields Thoroughbred dynasty, was purchased in April 1936. Nijinsky was born in February 1967. During the intervening thirty-one years the remarkable horses from this farm would have an unprecedented impact on Thoroughbred breeding. While all Thoroughbreds trace their ancestry in the male line to the Godolphin Arabian, Byerley Turk, or Darley Arabian, I might suggest that in the 21st century, the vast majority of Thoroughbreds trace their ancestry to mares and stallions of Windfields Farm.

How this came to be is a remarkable story, yet not widely known. The main reason, of course, is that it is a Canadian story. Canadians are a reticent people, not inclined to boast or trumpet our successes. But even if we were so inclined, in the early to middle 20th century, no one would have listened: How could Canadians raise Thoroughbreds, much less champion Thoroughbreds, in a country apparently under snow for most of the year? E.P. Taylor set out to do just that. And he succeeded.

It is a story I know very well. Windfields Farm became part of my life when I was fourteen and discovered that the original farm and all its beautiful horses, was just a half-hour bicycle ride from my home. I have seldom strayed far from Windfields since. I am continually drawn back, as if it is a magnet for my heart.

The sheer brilliance of Nijinsky moved some to glance, however briefly, at Canada as a source of special horses: for the most part, he was considered a fluke. It wasn't until several years later, when another Canadian son of Northern Dancer, The Minstrel, blasted to glory in the 1977 English Derby, that Canada, and specifically

Windfields Farm, and more specifically, Northern Dancer, were taken seriously.

In telling the story of Nijinsky for my Japanese readers, I found myself examining the evolution of Windfields through the stories of its brilliant Thoroughbred stars. I was writing at a healthy clip, enjoying the assignment, especially when the opportunity presented itself, to segue from the past to the present. For example, in the spring of 1999, when Charismatic won the Kentucky Derby, I was writing about the Windfields colt, New Providence, winning the 1959 Queen's Plate. Charismatic's sire, Summer Squall, is a great-grandson of New Providence. His other male-line great-grandfather is Nearctic, the focus of the mystery.

The mystery began as a casual question, a puzzle.

I was writing about Lyford Cay and Chopadette. Lyford Cay was owned by E.P. Taylor, Chopadette was owned by his wife, Winifred. The good-natured rivalry between husband and wife leading up to the 1957 Queen's Plate was often reported by sports writers. E.P. Taylor offered to buy a brand-new Cadillac for jockey, Avelino Gomez, if he won the Queen's Plate on Lyford Cay. He did. Mrs. Taylor's Chopadette was second. Avelino Gomez was soon driving a black Cadillac, the size of a yacht around the backstretch.

Both Lyford Cay and Chopadette were born of the Windfields foal crop of 1954, as was Nearctic. It was at this point I asked the question: what happened to Nearctic? I knew that Nearctic had raced as a two-year-old, winning stakes races in both Canada and the United States. Why then was he not a Queen's Plate candidate? The Queen's Plate is for three-year-old Canadian-born Thoroughbreds. Nearctic certainly qualified. He was owned by the Taylors, born and raised on their National Stud Farm in Oshawa, Ontario.

E.P. Taylor had gone to great lengths — and expense — to acquire Nearctic's mother, Lady Angela; and to even greater lengths and expense, to negotiate the mating that would produce Nearctic. Nearctic was, in fact, the best-bred Thoroughbred foaled in Canada.

For that matter, he was one of the most beautifully bred Thoroughbreds foaled anywhere, at any time. Nearctic had raced at two. He won four major races. Theoretically, Nearctic should not only have been a Queen's Plate candidate, but a contender.

Taylor was an enthusiastic monarchist. The Queen's Plate is abounding with ceremony and tradition, top hats and morning coats, lavish bonnets and horse-drawn landaus. A portion of the prize money comes straight from the coffers of the British monarchy. Having one of his horses win this race was very important to Taylor. And as Taylor had begun selling some of his yearlings a few years earlier, it made good business sense to showcase his horses in Canada's premier horse race.

Surely Nearctic, the most regally bred of Taylor's three-year-old horses, should have at least have been in the Queen's Plate prep races. So why wasn't he? I felt obligated to come up with an answer — both for myself and for my Japanese readers.

One of the interesting aspects of working for *Gallop* was that most of my Japanese readers were not very familiar with horse racing outside their own country whether bloodlines, locales, or personalities thus I frequently found myself offering some explanation or description. In the process I learned to question everything.

While writing for *Gallop*, I kept a photograph of the horse I was writing about on my desk. It helped me to keep focused. So, when I set out to write about Nearctic, I placed the photograph that is on the jacket cover, to the right of my computer. It wasn't long before I became captivated by the image of this beautiful, yet mysterious animal.

First I realized that my young horse, Val d'Argent, bore an uncanny resemblance to Nearctic: both have two hind white socks, and a dash of white on the forehead. Nearctic's marking looked like a check mark. Val's marking is in exactly the same spot—the same white slash—but without the little upswing at the end. But it is in body type and the way he carries himself that he is most similar to Nearctic. Val d'Argent has the lofty carriage that is the Nearctic trademark. Nijinsky also carried his head very high— as if scanning off into the distance above the crowd, aristocrats aware of their nobility. I saw that look with Royal Anthem and more recently with Fusaichi Pegasus.

Val d'Argent like his great great-grandfather, is an extremely sensitive and volatile animal. Some might say he is crazed. He certainly was when I first got him; he is also partly blind. It took two years to gain his trust. Simply leading him from his paddock to his stall was a challenge not everyone wanted to assume.

In those early days I worried a lot about Val d'Argent. I didn't want anyone else hurt by him. The horse had me stymied. I was anxious to find the key to this animal, and to understand his demons.

Val d'Argent led me into the past, beyond Northern Dancer to Nearctic. Like so many Canadians, I was a big Northern Dancer fan. No one I knew, except Windfields stallion manager, Harry Green, even mentioned Nearctic. (Harry's passion for Nearctic was considered merely one of Harry's many endearing quirks.)

I began to wonder if knowing more about Nearctic might help me with my horse. While I was at it, I would also clear up the mystery of Nearctic's disappearance during the first half of his three-year-old year.

I began my research at Windfields Farm. Office manager, Loraine O'Brien, had catalogued, filed, and stored every scrap of paper relating to the place in large cardboard filing boxes in a locked room above the old stud barn. On the top of each box Loraine methodically listed its contents. She had numbered the boxes and had organized a master list. Loraine looked up Nearctic and the corresponding box number and off we went. Simple.

It seems however, that the person who hauled these heavy boxes up the narrow staircase and deposited them in the storeroom, lacked Loraine's organizational skills. The boxes were stacked to the ceiling and in no particular order. So it didn't immediately help that the number and the sheet outlining the contents were on the top of each box. Perhaps it was assumed that no one would ever want to access the information contained in the boxes; perhaps no one was meant to.

So it was that I spent one summer afternoon climbing over, under and around stacks of boxes. Hauling them off the shelves, hoisting them back up. Since I was writing about Nijinsky at the time, I thought I might find additional data on his dam, Flaming Page; her sire, Bull Page; Nearctic's full-brother, Empire Day; and a few others. I created a list and kept moving boxes.

The room was small and hot, the air was close and stale, tasting like old papers. After several hours I had come up with one slim file folder containing Nearctic's registration, the cover of the June 1959 U.S. Jockey Club *Racing Calendar* featuring a photo of Nearctic, and copies of a couple of press clippings. I found nothing on the other horses that I did not already know. I telephoned Bill Talon, editor of the *Daily Racing Form* and asked permission to use their library. Nearctic raced from 1956 to 1959. The information from this era is neither on microfilm nor computer; but in copies of the *Daily Racing Form*, bound into giant books each weighing at least twenty pounds.

I stopped by Talon's office en route to the library at the back of the *Daily Racing Form* offices and optimistically assured him that it should not take long to find what I was looking for.

It wasn't long before I found myself lured into a convoluted maze of highly questionable events and circumstances. As the story of Nearctic began to take shape and I soon understood why great chunks of the story had vanished or been buried.

I went through every *Daily Racing Form* of the four-year period that Nearctic raced—page by page. Because of the bulk of these bound editions, and the fragile condition of the paper, I was not able to photocopy anything; but I made notes of every mention of Nearctic: past performance charts, columnists, reporters. These notes formed the skeleton of *Dark Horse.*

I was in the *Daily Racing Form* library so frequently that one day as I walked past Talon's office, he shouted, "Where were you yesterday? Why didn't you show up for work? I might have to dock your pay."

In the meantime I continued spending time with Val d'Argent. Trying to work with him, to understand him. At first he was so pumped with nervous energy that touching him was almost like sticking your finger in a socket. He could not abide anyone being close. Being in the stall with him was often unnerving. Unpredictable, volatile, you never knew when he was going to strike next.

I didn't expect Val d'Argent to be placid—he is after all, a highly-bred Thoroughbred. One of the fundamental elements that distinguishes this hybrid horse is its nervous energy. Still, Val d'Argent was more combustible than most. That led me to reread Federico Tesio's *Breeding the Racehorse* and, in particular, his theories on nervous energy.

That, in turn, led me to an article by John Aiscan in an 1973 issue of the *British Racehorse.* Aiscan asserts that Nearctic resembles his sire, Nearco, more than any of Nearco's sons. Aiscan also shows that of all the horses sharing Nearctic's gene base—those resulting from breeding Nearco to a daughter of Hyperion—Nearctic is the only one to prevail. His conclusion is that the genetic mix was simply too combustible. Val d'Argent certainly had inherited this explosiveness. My next question was: why Nearctic was the only one of all those horses to endure? Was it possible that Pete McCann had something to do with this?

Pete was the trainer of Windfields Farm racehorses at the time of Nearctic. Pete seemed to have the best rapport, and certainly the most success, with Nearctic. Yet the horse was often shipped off to other trainers. Why? It didn't make sense.

I tracked down Pete's daughter, Reta McCann Irwin, who told

me that Pete was in his nineties and living a very reclusive existence on a farm northeast of Toronto. Reta and her husband, Martin, visited Pete every Sunday. Through considerable persuasion on the part of Reta, Pete eventually agreed to see me, but at the last minute, changed his mind.

According to Reta, Pete was concerned about what he might say. At the time, I assumed Pete was simply being as bashful and uncommunicative as he always had been. I assured Reta I only wanted to know about Nearctic, not about the way the horse was handled. I promised I would *not* quote Pete directly about what happened with Nearctic. It would not be an interview, simply a conversation.

I look back and wonder "what was I thinking?"

When I began to piece together the story of Nearctic, I had no idea how badly the horse had been handled, nor how and why parts of this story had been swept under the rug. I did not understand Pete's reluctance to speak to me about Nearctic, nor did I know how painful it would be for him.

I continued leafing through Nearctic's past at the *Daily Racing Form* office. Parts of the story were decidedly unpleasant. I didn't like what I was discovering, but I had to continue. As I was becoming quite miserable, Reta phoned, inviting me to a McCann family reunion that she and Scott Brown, one of Pete's grandchildren, were organizing. The event would be held at Scott's home in Markham, Ontario, not far from the Markham Fairgrounds, where Pete began his long and distinguished career with horses. They also invited Beth Heriot, E.P. Taylor's long-time executive assistant. There was, however, no guarantee that Pete would show up. Chances were he would cancel, as he had already informed his family that he would not be attending Scott's wedding scheduled for several months later.

On the morning of the McCann family reunion I picked up Beth Heriot and off we went. On our way Beth reminded me of the time Windfields Farm racing manager, Joe Thomas, told E.P. Taylor that

Pete was sixty-five years old and wanted to retire from training at Windfields. Beth had overheard the conversation and, when Joe left, she marched into Taylor's office and set the record straight.

"I told Mr. Taylor that nothing was further from the truth. Pete did *not* want to retire," she recalled. "And I reminded Mr. Taylor that Pete was the best horse trainer in the country." Beth added that Pete would probably go on training horses well into his eighties, and that Taylor should not harbour any thoughts about forcing Pete into retiring.

Pete continued training Windfields Farm Thoroughbreds.

Five years later, however, Thomas got his way—sort of. Late in the Fall of 1968, Joe Thomas announced that, as he would be celebrating his seventieth birthday the following year, Pete would be retiring. Thomas dispersed the Windfields horses among five or six public trainers.

However, as Beth Heriot had predicted, Pete had no intention of retiring. Ever. Although, nearing his ninetieth birthday, Pete quit riding, he continued to care for a couple of Thoroughbreds until several days before he died.

As we neared Markham, Beth and I bet on whether Pete would appear at the reunion. Beth had known Pete since the 1950s; she was wagering that, at the last minute, he would decide against coming. I tended to agree, but held a glimmer of hope that I would get to see him.

And there he was! He seemed smaller than I remembered. But, I told myself, I had not seen him for more than ten years. Then I realized that most often when I had seen him in the past, he was on the back of a horse. And that was part of Pete's artistry: He rode the horses he trained.

The reunion had brought out quite a crowd, including two of Pete's three daughters, grandchildren, spouses, great-grandchildren. But at the centre were Pete and Beth. They had not seen each other for many, many years, and it was immediately apparent that they were both glad of this reunion.

I sat in one corner of the room with Pete and Beth. The extended McCann clan sat facing us, like an audience. They seemed as anxious as I to find out more about Pete and Nearctic.

It didn't happen. I didn't have to worry about my promise not to quote Pete on the subject of Nearctic. When the conversation turned to this one horse, Pete changed the subject. I should not have been surprised.

When I reminded Pete that he once told me that Nearctic "had a mean streak, that the good ones often do," he simply said, "Oh, Nearctic was a nice horse." Trying to get information about Nearctic from Pete was going to be like wringing water out of a dry towel.

Still I soldiered on.

"Well, Nearctic must have been pretty tough to have survived all that he was put through," said I.

"Bunty Lawless, now there was a tough horse," replied Pete.

Like a horse that didn't want to cross a stream, every time I led him to the subject of Nearctic, Pete balked and bolted off in another direction. I had to admire his determination, which is no doubt one of the reasons he was able to get along with Nearctic.

I too am very determined. I had done a lot of pleading, reasoning and cajoling to have this opportunity to speak to the man who knew Nearctic, and I was aware that I might not get another. I was not prepared to back down. Nor was he. But by listening very carefully, I was able to glean snippets of information here and there.

That afternoon, Pete offered me insights into his own nature, and thereby glimpses into his enormous ability with horses, especially horses like Nearctic. Pete did not believe in fighting a horse. He figured that there was no point to using up your energy, nor that of the animal, in a battle. One way he avoided a confrontation was to employ a diversion—and Pete was certainly using diversionary methods on me. When I asked him about Nearctic, he talked about Bunty Lawless, and I listened.

I didn't realize that he had ridden Bunty Lawless. Apparently he had, in the mornings as an exercise rider, and then later as his trainer. (I had to go back to the record books and find out for myself.) I discovered that Bunty Lawless won the Canadian International Stakes twice. I knew about the first time, in 1938, the inaugural year of this major horse-racing fixture. Bunty Lawless was a three-year-old. His trainer then was J. Anderson. E.P. Taylor's great filly, Mona Bell, was third that day. Three years later, Bunty Lawless won the Canadian International again. His trainer, this time, was Pete. Nearctic, Canadiana, Victoria Park, Viceregal, New Providence, Northern Dancer, Vice Regent. And now, Bunty Lawless. What great Canadian Thoroughbred had not benefitted from Pete's magical touch?

I was fascinated by what Pete had to say about Bunty Lawless — until I remembered my mission, and back I would go to Nearctic. I brought Pete up to date on the colossal influence of Nearctic as a stallion. He listened. He smiled.

"Nearctic must have been very special," said I.

"Now Viceregal, now there was a horse that was *special*," responded Pete. His pale blue eyes lit up at the mention of Viceregal. His grandson Scott brought out an ancient photo album. There were photographs of Pete riding Viceregal. Pete beamed. So did I. Viceregal was so beautiful. Once again I became captivated by his memories.

Eventually I realized that a pattern was emerging. Pete was a master horse trainer, a master of diversionary tactics. And at ninety-something years old, his instincts, honed over so many decades, so many great Thoroughbreds, continued to be sharp and shrewd.

If this had been a game, Pete, was surely the winner. The dance may have been my idea, but he led every step of the way.

Still, I learned a great deal. Not about Nearctic, but about the man, who appears to have brought out the best in Nearctic and, I suspect, was responsible for this grand horse's survival.

I learned that when he was a young man, Pete left Canada with $6.25 in his pocket and hitchhiked to Cuba. Pete became the leading rider in Cuba and then became implicated in some sort of betting ring, and was suspended from race riding in Cuba. The memory of being heckled by the angry Spanish-speaking crowd still rang in his ears all these decades later. He came home, but returned to Cuba eleven months later to clear his name. Pete, the jockey, was reinstated.

I also learned that at eighteen Pete had been a champion flyweight boxer. And I have wondered, if his own innate toughness was a factor in his ability to handle the ever-volatile Nearctic. Pete was not a violent man. According to his children, Pete's father, the local police chief, was. Shy and passive, Pete, appears the antithesis of his father.

Pete was never a big man and now his size was diminished by age. Still, his hands were huge. It was easy to see that he might have been a fighter. So was Nearctic. I have come to believe that were it not for their peculiar symbiosis, the modern Thoroughbred would be very, very different.

Still, I could not prove it. Many of the people who could have helped had died—like Harry Green, E.P. Taylor, and Winifred Taylor. Some did speak but remembered little. Others recalled the "official" version of the story, the one I had accepted before embarking upon my research. Some didn't call me back. And Pete wouldn't talk.

I was, discouraged. I had done so much research, spent so much time, but I knew that *Dark Horse* lacked the richness, the authenticity of someone who had been there.

Then along came Bill Reeves. He had been Pete's assistant for about fifteen years, but not during the time of Nearctic. Nonetheless, I tracked him down in Maryland. When I told him that I was writing a book about Nearctic, his first reaction was, "Great! It's about time!"

It was as if he had been waiting for me to show up at the door.

For the next several weeks I spoke with Bill almost every day—at 11:30 a.m., after he came home from playing golf. Bill remembered so many of the details that have breathed life into this story.

Bill Reeves had been at Windfields during the Nearctic years, as broodmare manager. He was with Lady Angela when Nearctic was born. And, in the off-season, Reeves, a former jockey, joined the troop of exercise riders that helped Pete with the yearlings — among them, Nearctic.

PART ONE

THE ROAD TO NEARCTIC

The saga began when Edward "E.P." Taylor purchased Colonel R.S. McLaughlin's Parkwood Stables, a four-hundred-and-fifty acre horse farm near Oshawa, Ontario. Taylor had had no intention of buying Colonel McLaughlin's farm; he had no intention of breeding horses, much less champion Thoroughbreds.

It seems, however, that Taylor was lured by a succession of exceptional horses.

The first to capture Taylor's imagination was Sir Barton, a rangy chestnut colt owned by Commander J.K.L. Ross, a prominent Montreal sportsman. Sir Barton was front-page news in Montreal when he won the 1919 Kentucky Derby. Young Edward Taylor had ventured to Montreal just months prior to all this excitement to study engineering at McGill University. Sir Barton, the home-town hero, went on to win the Preakness and the Belmont Stakes—the first horse to earn the U.S. Triple Crown.

Taylor was born and raised in Ottawa, a rather conservative government town. Montreal, an eclectic mixture of French and English cultures was vibrant, cosmopolitan and daring—after all, this was the roaring twenties. By all accounts Taylor became enchanted with Montreal, particularly its horse racing. There were seven racetracks in the Montreal area, the most prestigious being Bluebonnets at the foot of Mount Royal, where the elite of Montreal's society was found strolling the manicured lawns of the members' enclosure.

Instead of returning home to Ottawa for summer vacation, Taylor found employment in Montreal so that he could indulge himself in his newfound passion of horse racing. During this time, while working as a toolmaker's apprentice, he invented the first electric toaster to brown both sides of a piece of bread at the same time. Taylor was eighteen years old.

He sold the rights to manufacture his invention and received a royalty for every "household toaster" sold. The income from this enterprise helped defray his university expenses and his frequent sojourns to Montreal's racetracks.

Taylor graduated from McGill with a degree in mechanical engineering and a passion for horses. He never practised as an engineer, but horses, particularly Thoroughbreds, would remain the focus of his life.

Taylor was the consummate entrepreneur. He was creative, charming, optimistic and restless—ever eager for new challenges. Before he was thirty he had: started up and sold a bus company, then a taxi company; worked his way from bond salesman to partner in a brokerage firm; and incorporated the Brewing Corporation of Ontario, which would become the cornerstone of his wealth.

In the wake of the 1929 stock market crash he set out to acquire and merge the almost forty breweries scattered throughout Ontario. In the spring of 1936, he got the idea for a second merger, of his business interests and his passion for Thoroughbred horse racing.

After he and his bride, Winifred, moved to Toronto in 1928, they frequently attended the races at one of the many Toronto-area tracks and Taylor longed to have racehorses of his own. But he had neither the time nor the money to devote to a racing stable. Part of his difficulty was that he was legally prohibited from advertising beer. This, he believed, dampened sales.

Taylor's solution was to start a small racing stable and name it Cosgrave after one of his newly acquired breweries. The Ontario Jockey Club secretary suggested he find a good trainer and recommended Bert Alexandra.

Bert Alexandra however, was through with training horses. His early and voluntary retirement was sparked by a battle with his former clients, the Coulter brothers. Bert also hated Canada's racetrack bureaucracy.

The son of an English horse trainer, Bert Alexandra was raised on racetracks. He rode his first winner in Tijuana, Mexico when he was thirteen years old. Over the years Bert had gained the reputation as one of continent's shrewdest "halter men," racetrack jargon for someone adept at picking up horses from claiming races, which account for about 75 per cent of Thoroughbred races in North America. The claiming race was designed to ensure that horses of comparable ability are competing against one another. The top horses are found in stakes, handicap or allowance races. Eligibility in a stakes race depends on nomination payments that may begin soon after the foal is born, and can become high. The theory is that owners will only continue nomination payments as long as they feel the horse shows promise of returning some of their investment.

In a claiming race, however, the onus is on the owner and/or trainer to determine the value of a horse and run it against horses deemed to be of similar value. To insure against someone entering a fifty-thousand-dollar horse as a sure win in a race for twenty-thousand-dollar horses, horses in claiming races may be purchased by another owner or trainer for the designated "value" of the race.

Claiming horses was Bert Alexandra's forte. People around the tracks hoped that if they didn't claim any horses from Bert, then he wouldn't take any from them. Many were actually afraid to claim from him for fear of attracting his attention to their stable. It didn't really matter. Bert would have claimed a horse from his grandmother.

Once, in Chicago, Bert Alexandra unknowingly claimed a horse owned by crime boss, Al Capone. That evening friends helped get Bert's horses on the first train out of Chicago. Bert hid on the same train.

At age thirty-three, he was quitting the racing game, a very successful and wealthy young man. Nonetheless, on Saturday afternoon, 25 April, 1936, Bert found himself driving into Toronto to meet some fellow who wanted to start a racing stable. The address he had been given was 496 Queen Street East, just west of the Don River. This slum, with shabby row housing and unsightly industrial plants seemed an unlikely district to find a new horse owner.

496 Queen Street East looked as though three buildings of varying size and height had been strapped together by the dingy, grey brick facade. All that interrupted the flat, lifeless face were a number of small windows, a loading dock and, in the centre, a tall open archway. At the police call-box across the road, a constable was attempting to keep a drunk upright while he called the local police station.

Bert Alexandra steered his automobile through the archway into an open courtyard and parked it by what appeared once to have been the stable area, now converted to garages. He was greeted by a charming young man in his mid-thirties, who introduced himself as Eddie Taylor. The pair made their way across the courtyard toward the business offices. Physically the two men presented a lively contrast. Of medium height and lean frame, with fine features, dark hair and dark complexion, Bert Alexandra was often referred to around the track as "The English Gypsy." Edward Taylor was tall, blond and handsome with broad shoulders and the physique of a professional athlete.

Taylor's office was small, dismal and sparsely furnished. Forty years later, Bert still remembered being puzzled why someone in such dire straits would even consider an expensive hobby like Thoroughbred racing.

Taylor got right to the point: "Bert, I'm interested in building a very large racing stable."

In view of the surroundings, this idea seemed quite mad. Nonetheless, Bert decided to hear what the fellow had to say.

"There is one drawback," Taylor continued. "I don't have any money."

This scarcely came as a great surprise. Alexandra didn't say anything, but recalls thinking, "How in hell does this man think he is going to build a big racing stable without any money?"

Alexandra drew a deep breath, and looked him straight in the eye: "Well, sir, how much can you afford to give me to start this stable with?"

"The very best I can get you is four thousand dollars," was the immediate reply.

The room was silent. Bert stroked his chin and shook his head a few times. He could stand up, wish the young man luck and return to his retirement. But, Bert Alexandra was intrigued by this unusual situation.

He couldn't quite put his finger on it, but there was something about the man that made Bert Alexandra sense that not only did Taylor believe he could build that "very large racing stable," but he might just do it.

Young Edward Taylor was a longshot, but he appealed to Bert's sense of devilment.

And, Bert Alexandra was one heck of a horse dealer. Before the meeting had adjourned, he had not only agreed to take Taylor's four thousand dollars, he had sold him one of his own horses, Madfest, for an additional thousand dollars and a percentage from his first two wins.

The following Monday afternoon, 27 April, Taylor received a telegram congratulating him and his new racing colours on their first victory. He read the message several times before concluding that his new horse trainer must be either drunk or crazy. After all, he had only met the man two days earlier.

He tracked down Bert by phone in Maryland: "Bert, it's Eddie Taylor. I can't understand your telegram. You could only have left town yesterday and today you're congratulating me on winning. I don't understand..."

"You won the second race of the day with a horse called Annimessic!" replied the Englishman. "You have got six horses in your stable now."

"Six!"

"There's Madfest, the horse I sold you on Saturday," explained Alexandra. "And I bought five horses here today in Maryland. In fact, four of the five won."

"Bert I still don't understand. All I gave you was four thousand dollars..."

"Correction!" Alexandra barked. "All I got for it in American money was thirty-six hundred dollars. There was four hundred dollars exchange."

"Well, whatever I gave you, how is it we have all these horses?" Before Bert Alexandra could answer, Edward Taylor announced: "I don't know what this is all about, but I will be at the racetrack tomorrow morning."

From the outset Edward Taylor and Bert Alexandra were an unlikely combination. Where Bert was a charming scoundrel, brimming with mischief, Edward Taylor was all decorum and propriety.

His wife, Winifred, however, had a marvellous sense of humour and it was her stories and comical anecdotes that first sent me off in search of Bert Alexandra. I eventually found him and his wife, Bea, living in Florida. Moored at the foot of their property was a grand sailboat named Carefree, after Alexandra's favourite racehorse.

Winifred Taylor referred to Bert Alexandra as "the gypsy," always with a smile. Taylor called him his "banker." Bert was never without a thousand-dollar roll in his pocket secured with a large blanket pin.

At the racetrack these two men would bet "hats" on anything from the outcome of a race to the date of their first meeting. Bert Alexandra won enough hypothetical hats to open up a haberdashery.

One afternoon in the late 1970s, I had lunch at Toronto's Woodbine racetrack with these two characters. They were both in their seventies and still arguing about the amount of Taylor's original investment back in April 1936.

At one point Taylor said, "You mustn't believe a man who doesn't work for a living," alluding to the fact that after fifteen years as Taylor's trainer, Bert Alexandra retired, this time permanently.

The morning after his initial meeting with Taylor, Alexandra headed for Maryland's Pimlico Park racetrack. He reached his destination at eight o'clock Monday morning.

It was a rule at Pimlico that in order to claim a horse, a person had to have started a horse at the Pimlico meet. This regulation was designed to deter non-local horsemen from depleting the racing stock and taking their horses elsewhere to race. Which was precisely what Bert Alexandra intended to do.

He had left Madfest back in Toronto, so he didn't have a horse to start at Pimlico. This meant he would have to bend the rules to buy one at the Maryland track. His plan to collect a string of horses for his new client hinged on getting a horse to start in a race, thereby making him eligible to claim further horses. It didn't matter what kind of a horse it was, as long as it could go from wire to wire. As luck would have it, in the backstretch at Pimlico, Bert came across an acquaintance and asked if he had a horse to sell.

"Sure," was the reply. "I've got Annimessic running in the second race this afternoon. Six hundred cash, and six hundred when he wins."

"Sounds all right," replied Alexandra. "Can the horse walk?"

When the fellow assured him the horse was sound in wind and limb, Bert undid the blanket pin that secured his pocket, and peeled off six one-hundred-dollar bills from his roll.

Bert drove directly to the barns and led the horse out of his stall to check him over. His acquaintance had not lied, Annimessic could walk, but with considerable difficulty. The horse's cracked hooves were so long that they had grown out and over his horseshoes. Bert estimated that the horse had been wearing these same shoes for months.

He put Annimessic back in his stall and went off in search of a blacksmith. The blacksmith pulled off the old shoes, trimmed the horse's hooves down and put on new shoes. Annimessic won the second race at Pimlico that afternoon, and Bert Alexandra spent the rest of the day looking at horses, studying past-performance charts and filing claiming slips. The master halter man was in his element.

Taylor had no idea what he was getting himself into when he hired Bert Alexandra. When he arrived at Pimlico the day after he received Alexandra's telegram, he was taken on a guided tour of his newly acquired string of Thoroughbreds. One by one the horses were paraded out of their stalls, as Bert delivered an animated summary of each animal's bloodlines, past performances and racing potential.

Among the horses Taylor was introduced to was Jack Patches, a fifteen-hundred-dollar purchase that would be the leading handicap horse in Canada for three years; and to Nandi, the mare that would go on to produce Windfields, the first good horse bred by the Taylors.

Taylor realized he would not have the time to supervise his racing stable, so he appointed James Cosgrave to manage things. Formerly president of Cosgrave Brewery, and now an executive in Taylor's Brewing Corporation of Ontario, Cosgrave was an avid sport and horse- racing enthusiast.

The new Cosgrave racing stable was out of the gate, and off and winning. In an article in the *Evening Telegram* entitled "Cosgrave Stable Has Remarkable Success," J.P. Fitzgerald gushed:

"Congratulations are certainly coming to Jimmie Cosgrave and his partner in the remarkable success of their horses in this their first full race meet... It is no mean feat for any stable to capture four races in as many starts and miss the fifth with the best horse in it by just one jump.... Goodness only knows what this combination of free-handed and aggressive owners with a capable and canny trainer like A.E. Alexandra may do before the summer is over."

While Taylor was frequently at the tracks, there is little mention of him in these early days, and James Cosgrave is the one partner photographed with the Cosgrave horses in the winner's circle. Taylor's aversion to publicity and his involvement in the Brewing Corporation encouraged a low profile. He did attend to the overall operations of the stable and, very occasionally, was compelled to buy a young horse with racing potential from a local breeder. The majority of the Cosgrave racehorses were, however, animals that Bert Alexandra had claimed at the track.

One of Taylor's early purchases was Mona Bell, a marvellous filly that surely captured his imagination. Mona Bell and the colt Bunty Lawless were two of the most important Canadian horses in this period. Taylor acquired Mona Bell as a yearling from a local breeder for six hundred dollars. The filly was by the imported stallion Osiris II out of the St. James mare, Belmona.

The story of how Toronto tavern owner, Willie Morrissey, came to own Bunty Lawless, is considerably more colourful. One afternoon Morrissey heard that Jack Whyte was selling a horse called Gift Roman for eight hundred dollars. It sounded like a good deal, so Morrissey gave a friend the cash and dispatched him to buy the horse.

When Jack Whyte discovered that the buyer would be Willie Morrissey, he raised the price to twelve hundred dollars. Morrissey, an Irishman with a contrary nature under the sunniest of skies, became obsessed with getting revenge.

The following week Morrissey noticed that Jack Whyte was running a filly called Mintwina in a two-thousand-dollar claiming race. Strictly for spite, Morrissey claimed Mintwina.

Morrissey's revenge was short-lived. The first time she raced in his colours Mintwina broke the sesamoid in her right forefoot. Morrissey's ferocious temper erupted once again. He was going to have the filly put to her death. Fortunately, Morrissey's friend, "Doc" Hodgson convinced him that Mintwina's life should be spared.

The filly was shipped to "Doc" Hodgson's farm, north of Toronto. Eventually Mintwina was able to walk and get around, but her racing days were over. "Doc" Hodgson thought she would be a good broodmare. Willie Morrissey had absolutely no interest in breeding Thoroughbreds, but "Doc" Hodgson persevered, and somehow persuaded Morrissey to have Mintwina bred to Frank Selke's stallion, Ladder. The result was Bunty Lawless.

Time and again Mona Bell and Bunty Lawless were pitted against each other on Ontario racecourses. Mona Bell was the best filly running in Canada at the time, but Bunty Lawless was the stronger racehorse. Still, Mona Bell beat Bunty Lawless on a number of occasions, with much of the credit going to her cunning trainer, Bert Alexandra.

Bert would learn in which races Morrissey entered Bunty Lawless and would then enter a number of the Cosgrave horses, including Mona Bell, in the same event. On the day of the race, Bert would withdraw his horses, so diminishing an already small field to a point that the event would be cancelled.

All the while, Bert would be preparing Mona Bell for a race several days later. As Bunty Lawless had missed his race, Morrissey would enter his colt in the contest Alexandra had chosen. By that time Bunty Lawless would be slightly off his conditioning, having been readied for the cancelled event, while Mona Bell would be in peak condition. Bert stole a number of races using this particular ploy.

It wasn't long before large colour photographs of Mona Bell were displayed on the walls of Ontario taverns. Beneath her photo, in bold letters was the word COSGRAVE. Edward Taylor had discovered a way to circumvent the province's law against advertising alcohol.

The rivalry between Mona Bell and Bunty Lawless was so well-publicized that when their owners declared, in the summer of 1939, that upon their retirement from racing the pair would be mated, the announcement made the headlines.

Sadly, that August, Mona Bell slipped on the muddy Stamford Park track and broke her leg. Taylor and Alexandra were desperate to save her, so she might live out her days as a broodmare. But there was no hope that she would walk again. Mona Bell was euthanized and buried in the infield of Stamford Park, not far from where the accident had occurred.

Until Mona Bell, Edward Taylor had no interest in breeding Thoroughbreds. When he and his wife built their Toronto estate, Taylor had a small, four-horse barn constructed on the property, quite close the house, to accommodate his riding horses. His racehorses were housed at the track. In the winter, Alexandra took the racehorses to train in California or Florida. Those horses that did not go south went to a local boarding stable.

It seems an appropriate memorial to Mona Bell, a courageous, determined filly, that she was the one to raise Edward Taylor's sights. She was special. And when she died, Edward Taylor wept.

Bunty Lawless was retired to stud in 1940. While saddened and disappointed by the death of Mona Bell, Taylor agreed that Nandi, one of the original five horses claimed by Bert Alexandra at Pimlico, be bred with Bunty Lawless. In the spring of 1942, Nandi gave birth to a filly, the first offspring sired by Bunty Lawless. When Nandi was bred back to Bunty Lawless, she produced a brown colt, which Winifred Taylor named Windfields after their Toronto estate.

In 1945 Windfields showed tremendous promise as a two-year-old, winning his first start, a four-furlong gallop, by six lengths. He then established a track record in the Victoria Stakes. And broke it in the Rosedale Purse. Windfields was then sidelined for the season by an injury.

That same year Taylor dissolved the Cosgrave racing stable. In future, the horses would run in the name of E.P. Taylor. In 1946 he was awarded his "turquoise and gold" racing silk life colours by the Jockey Club in New York.

Windfields spent the early part of his three-year-old season campaigning in New York State. This made him ineligible to run in Canada's most prestigious horse race, the King's Plate. The directors of the Ontario Jockey Club, a somewhat parochial lot, had originally restricted the race to horses bred and raced solely in Ontario.

However, in 1944, the Ontario Jockey Club directors opened the race to all Canadian-bred Thoroughbreds. They also declared that these horses were allowed to go to the United States, to train during the winter, but not race. Which is precisely what Windfields was doing, with considerable success.

That year, Colonel R.S. McLaughlin's Kingarvie won the King's

Plate by six lengths, splashing his way through the sloppy Woodbine track in a torrential downpour.

Canadian turf writers and racing fans alike began to speculate on whether Kingarvie or Windfields was the better horse. As Windfields was not racing in Canada, supporters of Kingarvie were convinced that Taylor was afraid of having his colt beaten by the reigning King's Plate winner.

One evening at a dinner party, Taylor was confronted by two ardent Kingarvie supporters. The ensuing banter resulted in some serious "play or pay" wagering, meaning that Taylor would have to pay up if he did not run Windfields against Kingarvie.

The next morning Taylor called Bert Alexandra at Belmont Park where he was racing Windfields:

"Bert, they're making my life miserable up here. Even the newspapers are saying that I am afraid to run Windfields against Kingarvie. We are going to have to bring him up here to run in the Breeders' Stakes."

Alexandra was reluctant. He despised the Ontario Jockey Club directors with a passion and Windfields had had an arduous winter campaign. Moreover, he argued, the Breeders' Stakes was only two days away.

"I know," said Taylor, "but they are calling me a coward as far as this horse is concerned."

"Okay, you own the horse. But we don't have much time."

"I realize that," concurred Taylor, "so you had better fly Windfields to Toronto."

Taylor had to go to Ottawa on business and Bert was left to look after Windfields' transportation. However, when Bert arrived at the airport with Windfields, he discovered that the headroom in the plane that was to fly the horse to Canada, was too confined. If Windfields were to become nervous on the flight and were to rear up, he would crack his head on the ceiling. As Bert didn't want to run Windfields in the Breeders' Stakes, he figured he had a perfect excuse. There was not time to trailer the horse back to Canada, so he returned Windfields to Belmont Park.

When Taylor phoned from Ottawa to make sure that Windfields had arrived safely, he was horrified to discover that his horse was still in New York. If Windfields did not show up for the race against Kingarvie, it would be perceived as an admission that Taylor felt his horse was no match against Kingarvie.

Taylor was a compelling and shrewd negotiator, a skill he had honed to perfection during the war, when he was posted to Washington D.C., where he was responsible for implementing the Hyde Park agreement, wherein Canada traded raw materials to the United States in return for products needed for the war effort. Later Winston Churchill appointed him head of the British Supply Council in the U.S., where he procured goods directly on behalf of Britain.

During that time he had met the president of American Airlines. Very few horses were transported by air in those days, but he knew that American Airlines had a plane that could be fitted for the job. So with precious little time before the race with Kingarvie, Taylor put in a phone call. The plane, he discovered, was in New York, but the special horse stalls were in California.

Taylor had American Airlines fly the plane to California, install the special stalls, return to New York and pick up Windfields. One hour and twenty minutes after the plane left Newark Airport, Windfields became the first horse to be flown into Canada. It was also the first time a DC-4 air freighter had landed at Toronto's Malton Airport and the ground crew were ill-prepared for the next hurdle—getting the horse off the plane. Eventually they pulled a large open truck alongside the plane, and Windfields was led out of the cargo bay to the truck and from there down a hastily-built ramp to the ground. Apparently the horse was far calmer than the humans.

The following day more than thirty thousand people gathered at Old Woodbine Park to witness the well-publicized showdown between Windfields and Kingarvie. Although Windfields had arrived only at six o'clock the previous evening and was not in top condition due to a demanding winter season in the United States, the fans had their money on Windfields.

He, however, wanted no part of it. First, he refused to go into the starting gate. Eventually the gate crew backed him in. The starting bell rang, the gates flew open, and Windfields ambled out of the gate.

Windfields then loped along, blissfully unaware of the dismay of his supporters, and particularly his owner, who had spent thousands to get him to Toronto, and a substantial amount in wagers both on and off the track.

At the half-mile pole Kingarvie, who had fallen coming out of the gate, galloped past Windfields, leaving Taylor's colt trailing the field. Bert had instructed Windfields' jockey not to use his whip on the colt, so there he sat as if on a pleasant canter in the park. Defeat was imminent. The crowd let out a collective groan.

Suddenly Windfields had a change of heart. In a single stride, he bounded from an easy canter to a turbo-charged gallop. In a blink he was alongside Kingarvie. In two, he cruised across the finish, five lengths ahead of second-place Kingarvie.

Taylor, who generally conducted himself with decorum, was euphoric. Never before had he experienced the build-up, the tension, prior to and during the race, and the very high stakes. And Windfields was *his* horse, one he had bred, not purchased. This sense of proprietorship and achievement was too seductive. Taylor was hooked.

Epic was a thrill of a different kind.

Foaled in 1946, Epic was the son of Taylor's mare, Fairy Imp, who had been bred to Bunty Lawless when she retired from racing. Winifred Taylor generally named the Windfields Farm horses, but her husband was determined to name this one.

"I spent a lot of time trying to find a name for this fellow," Taylor confided. "Finally I decided to thumb through the dictionary. Epic appealed to me, as it was short and easily remembered, an epic being a poem, or an *event of importance*."

Epic, was indeed an event of importance, he also won Canadian horse racing's event of importance, the King's Plate. Conducted under Royal patronage, the race is designated for the ruling monarch in Great Britain.

The "Plate" part of this royal race dates back to the seventeenth century, when Charles II, offered plates to the winners of horse races at Newmarket, England. The Plate races were originally conducted over four-mile heats and the horses were made to carry 12 stone (168 pounds). While there was a variety of regulations for horse races, the Plate races were the only ones with formal rules, as put forth by the King. It was Charles II's intention to create some order, along with encouraging the breeding of powerful and durable racehorses. Until the close of the 18th century, the horse best able to carry this huge burden to victory, over and over, was considered the ultimate Thoroughbred.

Canada held her first King's Plate in 1836 at Trois Rivières, then a small settlement in Lower Canada (Quebec). Twenty-three years later the Toronto Turf Club petitioned Queen Victoria to award a similar Plate for Thoroughbred racing in Canada West (Ontario). The Queen granted the request by splitting the annual purse of one hundred guineas originally presented to the Quebec horse race between the two provincial events. Quebec's Plate did not last long, but the Ontario race is now North America's oldest continually run sporting event.

The first Plate to be held under the auspices of the Toronto Turf Club was run in the village of Carleton, a five-mile carriage ride from Toronto, in 1860. More than four thousand of Toronto's forty-five thousand residents hitched up their horses and took to the dusty road for this inaugural running. The race was open to any Thoroughbred bred in Canada West (Ontario) that had not won a previous race; of the eight entries the five-year-old Don Juan emerged triumphant, winning two of the three one-mile heats.

Up to three months before the ninetieth running of the King's Plate in 1949 it was doubtful that Edward and Winifred Taylor's Epic would even make it to the starting gate. Epic had not been raced as a two-year-old because of his fragile ankles, and Bert Alexandra took the big rangy colt to California for a winter of conditioning in preparation for the King's Plate. In the spring of 1946, Bert shipped Epic to New York, to continue his training, and to Woodbine on 15 May to familiarize Epic with the track conditions. They arrived less than a week prior to the King's Plate Trials, but considering Bert's antipathy towards the Canadian Thoroughbred racing establishment, it is surprising that the horse showed up at all.

Early in the year, Bert had been quite pessimistic about Epic's chances, but his assistant, Johnny Collins, refused to give up on the colt. Epic responded to Collins' devotion; and by the time they arrived in Canada, Bert was telling all who would listen that Epic was by far the best horse in Canada. Local newspaper reporters listened with interest and soon the pre-race coverage featured Epic as a serious threat to the winter book favourite, Speedy Irish.

When Epic went on display in his first workout at five furlongs, a great crowd turned out for the event. A proud and confident Taylor led the brigade of clockers to time Epic's every stride. Three months earlier Taylor had told Canadian journalist, Joe Perlove, that if Epic made it to the starting gate, he would win the King's Plate; Perlove had dutifully reported the prediction to his readers. And on the morning of his first pre-Plate gallop, Epic looked every inch the champion.

On Saturday afternoon, 21 May 1946, opening day at Woodbine Park, Epic entered the first division of the King's Plate Trials. Although he broke slowly from the starting gate, he soon got his feet under him. Jockey Chris Rogers allowed the colt to coast along in a good position down the backstretch, and by the time the field had reached the homestretch, Epic had taken the lead to score his first victory with relative ease.

As Canada's champion two-year-old, Speedy Irish devastated all opposition in the second division of the King's Plate Trials. The forthcoming King's Plate was fast becoming a match race between these two Canadian-bred colts.

Bert had become so optimistic that every time he and Taylor spoke, Bert advised his employer to wager with anyone willing to bet on the outcome of the Plate, and the two men ended up with appreciable investments on Epic.

On the morning of the King's Plate all hell broke loose. Bert Alexandra learned that his horse had drawn a post position outside the regular starting gate. The Ontario Jockey Club owned a twelve-horse starting gate. As there were seventeen entries, Club officials decided to start five horses from outside the barrier.

Alexandra argued that to make the race fair, management should have all the horses break from the old open barrier, but his suggestion fell on deaf ears. Furious at the racing officials, he announced that Epic would be scratched, and stormed off in search of his employer.

Throughout their relationship Taylor and Alexandra had engaged in some very lively discussions, but never a quarrel. As they argued over whether Epic should be withdrawn, four other owners pulled their horses out of the race, thereby moving Epic up to the last stall of the starting gate. Now, only the thirteenth entry, Filsis, would start from outside the gate.

The pre-race publicity had enticed a record crowd of forty-two thousand to Woodbine Park for the event. They gave Speedy Irish a slight edge, sending him off at 6-5, while Epic went to the post at 7-5. As starter Doug Haig ushered the horses into the gate the anticipation made the grey, overcast day electrifying.

The sharp clang of the bell unleashed the thirteen horses. The tension mounted. Epic leapt from the gate, jockey Chris Rogers manoeuvered the colt into position about three lengths off pacesetter Bolaris, while Speedy Irish coasted along at the end of the pack. Epic wanted to run, so Rogers let his mount take the lead from a tiring Bolaris as they approached the eastern turn coming out of the backstretch. At the same time, Speedy Irish, famous for his last-minute drive, started to make his move. As the horses hit the homestretch, he was on the outside, flying.

This was the showdown everyone was waiting for. Speedy Irish had blasted his way from thirteenth to second place and the forty-two thousand fans were on their feet shouting and cheering their favourites over the final furlong. Although Speedy Irish had given his all, he failed to catch Epic.

Presentation of the purse was made on behalf of King George VI by the Governor-General of Canada, Field Marshall Earl Alexander of Tunis. After the introductions were made, an Ontario Jockey Club official explained that this was the first King's Plate victory for the owner, the first for the trainer, and the first for the jockey.

Bert Alexandra not only despised the Ontario Jockey Club, he intensely disliked all the ceremony in the winner's enclosure: it was the horse, not the people who won the race. Bert vehemently opposed the crowds who cram into the winner's enclosure to get their picture taken. In all his years of training horses, Bert Alexandra had never once had his photograph taken in the winner's enclosure with a horse. He was becoming more agitated by the second.

Just as the Ontario Jockey Club official completed his list of "firsts" for the Governor-General, and for the rest of Canada through the radio broadcast hookup, Bert sardonically shouted into the microphone, "And sir, it was the *first* for the horse!"

Thus, curiously, and prophetically, Epic had lived up to his name— *an event of importance.* He had given Taylor his first taste of the glamour and the excitement that comes from winning a prestigious horse race. Epic had also raised Taylor's sights; ultimately he and his horses would dominate Thoroughbred racing and breeding the world over.

When in the fall of 1950 Colonel Sam McLaughlin called Taylor and announced that he planned to sell Parkwood, Taylor responded that *he* certainly did not need another farm. Taylor and his wife had built a charming, elegant estate on about forty acres bordering Toronto's Bayview Avenue. Originally the land was bereft of trees, which inspired Winifred Taylor to name the estate Windfields. The property would have been more than adequate, had Taylor not been enticed into the breeding of Thoroughbreds.

The horses and the excitement they generated compelled Taylor to expand his original vision, and he had purchased property adjacent to their estate. Before long he had developed Windfields Farm into, if not the largest, certainly the most impressive and elaborate Thoroughbred farm in the country: thirty-eight broodmares, a considerable number of foals and yearlings, and two stallions, the U.S.-bred Illuminable and his own Windfields. The horses were housed in three large red-brick stables, and several smaller barns, in a maze of white fences.

It wasn't as if Taylor needed to keep busy. He was forty-nine years old and he in the prime of his business life. Through Argus Corporation, a holding company he had formed, his business activities were diverse and global. He frequently worked seven days a week. He organized and ran a hugely successful six-month campaign to restore and refurbish Toronto General Hospital. He also chaired fund-raising drives for the Victorian Order of Nurses and the Art Gallery of Ontario.

During the 1950s and 1960s, the Taylors had homes in Sussex, England; Chesapeake, Maryland; Oshawa and Toronto; four houses in the Bahamas; and apartments in Montreal, Quebec and New York City. They travelled from home to home in their private jet, painted turquoise and gold, Windfields Farm racing colours.

McLaughlin explained that although he had received offers from real estate developers, he was most anxious to have his property continue as a horse farm and, to that end, was prepared to make substantial price concessions.

Taylor promised McLaughlin that he would try to locate someone who was prepared to buy Parkwood and carry on its long Thoroughbred breeding tradition.

Born in 1871, Robert Samuel McLaughlin was a partner and chief designer at the McLaughlin Carriage Works, a family business started by his father. In 1908 the enterprise evolved into the McLaughlin Motor Car Company and began building Buick-powered McLaughlins and Chevrolets. Ten years later the company merged with the U.S. manufacturer, General Motors, to form General Motors of Canada with Sam McLaughlin as president until he retired in 1967.

When he decided to sell his farm, McLaughlin was nearing his eightieth birthday and felt that he could no longer cope with its demands. He had established Parkwood twenty-two years earlier on the lush green hills just north of his native town of Oshawa; under his guidance the farm had produced some of Canada's leading Thoroughbreds of the 1930s and 1940s.

Taylor telephoned his friend, François Dupré, who had a magnificent Thoroughbred farm in the Normandy region of France. Dupré occasionally brought horses from France to run in Canada and had at one time expressed an interest in having a farm in Canada. Taylor arranged for Dupré to come to Canada. They would meet McLaughlin for lunch to discuss Parkwood.

By the time the three men met, however, Dupré's wife had apparently talked him out of buying the farm. By then Taylor was as anxious as McLaughlin that Parkwood be spared from development. As they ended their meeting, he said to McLaughlin, "Give me forty-eight hours. I think I can find a solution."

His solution was to turn Parkwood into a breeding farm similar to the National Stud in England, solely for the purpose of improving the Canadian Thoroughbred breed.

Within two days Taylor had come up with commitments from nine friends and associates. He, too, would join the group, each would have a ten per cent interest in the operation. The offer, with the plan that Parkwood would be preserved for Thoroughbred breeding, was put to McLaughlin. He was delighted and accepted without hesitation.

By the following morning, however, Taylor had changed his mind.

When it came to business dealings, Taylor was characteristically methodical and thorough. He studied every aspect. If he decided to go ahead with a project, he never looked back. Yet, it was this change of heart that ultimately resulted in Nearctic and his kin, and changed the course of Thoroughbred horse racing.

After Taylor phoned McLaughlin with the group's proposal, he began to draft a business plan for his proposed National Stud. Normally, he would have done this well in advance, but in order to save Parkwood from becoming a housing development, he was compelled to act quickly.

The idea was a very good one, but surely ahead of its time. Canadian Thoroughbred breeders, for the most part, did not aspire to great heights, and were unlikely to share his aspirations to improve the Canadian breed. They would take a lot of convincing—and that would take a lot of time and money.

Taylor studied the ramifications long into the night. By morning he realized that it would not work. The projected financial losses would be staggering. Besides, he was not a great proponent of business partnerships. He was a leader, an innovator, not a person who functioned well on a committee.

So he let his friends off the hook and decided to buy the farm on his own. As he already had Windfields Farm, taking on a second farm was a huge undertaking—and a clear indication of the depth of Taylor's commitment to Thoroughbred racing and breeding.

In the ensuing negotiations, McLaughlin included everything on the farm except for his riding horse, several race horses, and about eighty head of very fat cattle. The pair bartered back and forth and eventually eighty very fat cattle were thrown into the deal.

Parkwood was certainly an exquisite showplace. It came complete with two hundred acres of paddocks, five horse barns, a half-mile training track, a massive indoor riding arena, an office, a fully-equipped dispensary, five houses for staff and a number of cattle barns.

Once the negotiations were completed, Taylor held a dispersal sale of all the stock on the farm (except the cattle), he changed the name from Parkwood to the National Stud, and hired local Thoroughbred breeding authority, Gil Darlington, to manage the farm. Harry Green, who had been looking after the stallions at Windfields Farm was appointed stallion manager of the National Stud. And Gil Darlington brought in Peter Poole, a young horseman from British Columbia, to assist in organizing the National Stud.

In order to encourage others to raise the standard of Canadian Thoroughbreds and thereby the quality of Canadian horse racing Taylor offered complete facilities for breeding, foaling, raising and training at a very reasonable cost. To provide further incentive to Canadian Thoroughbred breeders, he reduced the stud fees on the five stallions standing at his new National Stud Farm.

At the time, the average Canadian-bred Thoroughbred yearling was selling for about fifteen hundred dollars. There was no way Taylor could successfully operate the National Stud selling horses at this price.

He had studied the economics of breeding Thoroughbreds in North America and in Great Britain. One of his conclusions was that the mare dominates the genetic mix by as much as seventy-five per cent:

"With the greatest stallion in the world and a poor mare, you will get a poor horse. With an ordinary stallion and a great mare, your chances are considerably better. With a great stallion and a great mare, your chances are excellent."

For the National Stud to pay for itself, they were going to have to breed very good horses, horses capable of winning the Classics. To achieve this, Taylor was going to have to invest in the very finest Thoroughbred broodmares. And since the home of the Thoroughbred is Newmarket, England, this was where he would begin his quest for Thoroughbred greatness. To that end, he contacted the British Bloodstock Agency, where the young bloodstock agent George Blackwell was assigned to him.

A new era had begun.

"Look back into your mighty ancestors."
WILLIAM SHAKESPEARE, *KING HENRY V*

George Blackwell was a novice agent at the British Bloodstock Agency when his employer told him that he was going to be representing a new Canadian client. Apparently this Canadian had requested that the British Bloodstock Agency purchase, on his behalf, the best broodmare in the 1952 December Newmarket sale. Money was no object.

Blackwell diligently thumbed through the catalogue of all the horses entered in the December Sales. He checked and doubled checked every pedigree page very closely before contacting his new Canadian client.

There was, however, really no contest, Lady Angela's bloodlines were impeccable. Blackwell felt quite confident in recommending her.

"It was really no problem," recalled Blackwell, many years later, "Lady Angela was by far the best mare in the sale."

Lady Angela was eight years old. The blood of England's greatest Thoroughbred matriarchs coursed through her veins. She was also a daughter of Hyperion, winner of the 1933 English Derby at Epsom, and sire of a succession of brilliant mares, including Hydroplane II, dam of the gallant Citation, 1948 U.S. Triple Crown winner.

Taylor may have been prepared to buy Lady Angela, sight unseen, and at any cost because of Hydroplane II. If there was a "dream horse" in North America at the time, it was Citation. Taylor had seen him run, and win, the Belmont Stakes. A month later Taylor went to Kentucky and purchased a very expensive yearling son of Bull Lea, sire of Citation. Winifred Taylor named the colt Bull Page. Although Bull Page did not become the next Citation, he was a good racehorse, and a better stallion, sire of Canadian Triple Crown winner, New Providence, and Queen's Plate winner, Flaming Page, dam of Nijinsky.

Determining the very best mare in the Newmarket sale had been easy; but the second part of Blackwell's assignment—to buy the mare—was where things got very complicated.

Blackwell had not yet met his new Canadian client. He knew very little about the man, except that his name was E.P. Taylor and that he was rumoured to be extremely wealthy. All Blackwell's communications with Taylor had been by Transatlantic cable and telephone.

Blackwell informed Taylor that Lady Angela was likely to be very expensive. She was in foal to Nearco, who, with Lady Angela's sire, Hyperion, were considered the most distinguished Thoroughbred stallions in Great Britain, if not the world.

Taylor assured Blackwell that he would pay any amount for Lady Angela, on one condition: that Lady Angela remain in England to give birth to her foal, and then be bred back to Nearco before coming to Canada.

Not only did Taylor's request seem to make no sense to young George Blackwell, it also caused him considerable grief.

Breeding Nearco to a daughter of Hyperion, mixing the blood of these two great stallions seemed the perfect genetic formula. To that end, almost every British Thoroughbred horse breeder who owned a daughter of Hyperion sent the mare to be bred to Nearco. Oftentimes, over and over. Yet, other than Noory, the 1952 Irish Oaks winner, there was nothing to suggest that this theory had any merit.

Lady Angela had been mated with Nearco on two previous occasions. Her offspring, showed no great success on the racecourses. Both animals were difficult to handle and neither had a glorious racing career.

Lady Angela's first foal by Nearco was an apparently

temperamental filly called Mary Martin. Her second Nearco offspring, Gabriel, was no angel. The colt had been gelded early, which suggests that his handlers hoped to alleviate his aggressiveness. Gabriel won only one minor race.

Thus, Taylor's insistence that Lady Angela be bred, for the *fourth time*, to Nearco, made no sense, at least not rationally. Yet, Taylor's dogged insistence became *the* turning point in Thoroughbred history.

(Unfortunately, by the time it occurred to me to ask about this incredible decision, Taylor had died, as had the other two people who might have offered insight, Winifred Taylor and Taylor's long-time stallion manager, Harry Green.)

When George Blackwell retired from his lengthy and successful career as a British bloodstock agent, he moved to Lexington, Kentucky. He and his wife lived in a townhouse complex adjoining the Marriott Hotel, where many out-of-town buyers and sellers stayed during the Keeneland sales. During one of my research trips to Kentucky, while most of the other Marriott guests were off to the Keeneland sales arena to gamble millions on "baby stallions," or, they hoped, glean millions from their yearlings, I strolled over to Blackwell's townhouse. What a rollicking time was had as George Blackwell regaled us with his recollections of trying to purchase Lady Angela, laughing at the memories, and the absurdity of it all. His humour was contagious.

The conundrum created by this new Canadian client would have troubled the most seasoned agent at the British Bloodstock Agency. Blackwell, however, was a neophyte, which, perhaps, worked in his favour.

Blackwell explained to Taylor that his request for a return breeding to Nearco was an unusual sales requirement, and suggested that it might not be possible. Taylor assured him that he would not purchase Lady Angela otherwise.

So young George Blackwell approached Lady Angela's owner,

Martin Benson, the British bookmaker who, coincidentally, was the major shareholder in Nearco. Benson had purchased Nearco from his owner/breeder, Federico Tesio, after the grand black colt won his final race, the two-mile Grand Prix de Paris on 26 June 1938 at Longchamp. Benson paid £60,000 for Nearco, then the highest price paid for a Thoroughbred. When he brought the colt to England, Benson set out to sell breeding rights to Nearco, in order to cover the cost of the horse and no doubt, make a profit.

It came as no surprise to Blackwell when Benson simply said, "Absolutely not!" Benson offered no explanation. Many years later, Blackwell suggested that Martin Benson may have been reluctant to use one of his personal breeding rights to Nearco with any mare other than his own.

Blackwell immediately conveyed Benson's sentiments to Taylor, assuming that his new Canadian client would acquiesce and that would be the end of it.

He was, of course, wrong.

The first thing Blackwell would learn was that once Taylor had an idea, or a goal, it was virtually impossible to deflect him from his course. So when he told Taylor that there was no chance that Martin Benson would offer a return breeding to Nearco, "He told me, and quite emphatically, might I add," reminisced Blackwell, "that those were his terms. And that if I was unable to secure a return breeding, then he was no longer interested in purchasing the mare."

Poor George Blackwell. He truly wanted to make a good impression, both on his new Canadian client and on his new employers, the British Bloodstock agency; but Martin Benson had practically thrown him out of the house. Blackwell knew only that he was going to have to face Benson again, and he was not looking forward to the encounter.

Finally Blackwell screwed up his courage and telephoned Benson — who refused to speak to him. So Blackwell telephoned again. And again.

"Eventually, and I must say, reluctantly, Martin Benson agreed to see me," recalled Blackwell. "But he advised me that he was firmly opposed to the idea of the return breeding to Lady Angela."

As Blackwell relived the events surrounding this turning point in Thoroughbred history, he was still somewhat incredulous that things actually worked out:

"Martin Benson had truly dug his heels in. Finally I told him that this Canadian was very wealthy. Very, very wealthy. In fact, I told Martin Benson that I understood Taylor was the wealthiest man in all of Canada and that he was committed to building an extensive Thoroughbred stud farm. So I suggested that his cooperation might be good for future horse sales."

Benson saw the logic of Blackwell's argument, but he was not convinced. Still, to Blackwell's relief, Benson said he would think about it, although he left Blackwell with the impression that it was highly unlikely that he would change his mind.

There was nothing left for Blackwell to do but wait.

Several days later Benson contacted him.

In order to escape England's cold, damp winters Benson annually migrated to Florida's warm weather and sunny skies. He lived the life of the very wealthy at home in England; elsewhere, however, it was a different matter. In the early 1950s, Great Britain had stringent currency controls, and the amount of money he was allowed to take out of the country was severely limited.

Perhaps, Benson suggested, this wealthy Canadian client might be prepared, not only to pay a vast sum for Lady Angela, but also provide him with additional spending money for his forthcoming Florida excursion.

"I wasn't sure how Taylor would react to this latest development," recalled Blackwell. "While I didn't know that what Martin Benson was requesting was *against* the law pertaining to currency controls, it no doubt *circumvented* the law. So I thought I had better explain that to Taylor."

"But when I told him, he said, 'As long as I personally am not doing anything illegal, I have no problem with this arrangement.'"

"I think the amount they finally settled upon was $3,000 in U.S. currency. It doesn't sound like a lot, but at the time, in the early fifties, it was substantial."

That did it. Blackwell paid $35,000 for Lady Angela on behalf of E.P. Taylor, at the 1952 December Sales at Newmarket. It was a colossal sum to pay for a Thoroughbred broodmare, even one with such a distinguished family tree. Especially one who had not given birth to a champion racehorse. At least not yet.

It is hard to imagine a Thoroughbred with a more magnificent ancestry than that of Nearctic. Through his dam, Lady Angela, Nearctic was born of a succession of some of the greatest matriarchs leading back to one of the original distinguished foundation mares, Old Bald Peg.

Lady Angela was not a particularly inspired racehorse. She was sent to the post seven times. She finished second in three minor events — the Ruth Woods Stakes, the Tisbury Purse and the Cowden Purse. Her sole victory was in the one-mile August Plate, a maiden three-year-old race at Epsom. Shortly thereafter she was retired to Martin Benson's Beech House Stud.

While Benson may have been disappointed by her lack of enthusiasm for racing, he must have held great hopes for Lady Angela as a broodmare. Through her sire, Hyperion, Lady Angela was of the blood of Selene, Pilgrim, Canterbury Pilgrim, Gondolette— some of the greatest broodmares in history. Lady Angela's maternal line is also extremely dynamic. Her dam, Sister Sarah, is a great-granddaughter of Pretty Polly, the sensational racehorse and Thoroughbred matriarch.

Bred and born in Ireland in 1901, Pretty Polly was owned by Major Eustace Loder. As a yearling, Pretty Polly was shipped by boat to England and then by horse box to Newmarket, where she went into training under the care of Peter Purcell Gilpin.

Pretty Polly made her first start in the British Dominion Two-Year-Old Plate, in June 1903, at England's Sandown Park. The official records say that she won the race by ten lengths. The unofficial word is that she won by close to one hundred yards!

Pretty Polly ran eight more times that year and coasted to victory each time. The following year she won the English One Thousand Guineas Stakes, the Coronation Stakes, the Nassau Stakes, and the St. Leger Stakes. Two days after the almost-two-mile St. Leger Stakes, Pretty Polly won the Park Hill Stakes.

By then Pretty Polly had a huge and enthusiastic following. The British media deemed her invincible. And so it was that Pretty Polly's handlers decided to ferry her across the English Channel and add some foreign currency to her earnings.

The chosen race was the Prix Conseil Municipal. And here, on French soil, Pretty Polly was beaten to the wire for the first time in her racing life. The winner was a 66-1 longshot: Presto prevailed over Pretty Polly by two-and-a-half lengths. Numerous excuses were offered: her journey to Paris was traumatic; the footing in France was soft and heavy; and her regular jockey, William Lane, had been injured and had to be replaced.

Pretty Polly returned to England—and to her winning ways. In the latter part of October she won the Free Handicap at Newmarket in a romp.

She raced and won four times as a four-year-old: the Coronation Cup, the Champion Stakes, the Jockey Club Gold Cup, and a match race. Her owners kept Pretty Polly in training as a five-year-old, as they had the Ascot Gold Cup in their sights.

Pretty Polly arrived triumphant at the Royal race meeting at Ascot Park in the summer of 1906. She had strolled to easy victories in her only two starts of the year, the March Stakes at Newmarket, and again, the Coronation Cup at Epsom, where she beat a worthy field that included the 1904 English Derby winner, St. Amant.

A vast crowd of Pretty Polly's admirers travelled to Ascot to see her prevail over her four opponents in the Ascot Gold Cup, a staggeringly long distance of two-and-a-half miles. The only other time Pretty Polly had raced over a distance longer than two miles was in the Jockey Club Cup at Newmarket in November 1905. In the closing seconds of the race, Bachelor's Button managed to get his head up to her flanks, but his efforts came too late, and Pretty Polly crossed the finish line first.

While not considered a Classic horse, Bachelor's Button had won a decent number of good races, including the 1904 Champion Stakes and the 1905 Doncaster Cup. He was seven years old, durable, and arrived at Ascot Park having just won the Manchester Cup. Bachelor's Button and the 1905 English Derby winner, Cicero, at 7-1, were joint second favourites.

No one wanted to bet against Pretty Polly.

There had been rumours that Pretty Polly might not even start in the Ascot Gold Cup. In early June, around the time she won the Coronation Cup, a wart-like, fungal growth had appeared on her belly, just behind her forelegs. The growth had been lanced long before the Ascot Gold Cup, but as it had been in the area touched by the girth, there was good cause for concern.

When Pretty Polly was led into Ascot's paddock area, there was further cause for concern: she was awash in sweat and appeared to be highly and uncharacteristically distressed.

St. Denis, winner of the Princess of Wales's Stakes and third in the 1904 English Derby was in the race solely as pacemaker for Bachelor's Button. Everyone knew of his assignment, and thus gave him odds of 500-1.

St. Denis established a strong lead as the small field galloped past the overflowing stands. It was a bright, sunny and brutally hot afternoon.

Achilles, a three-year-old colt, settled into second place with English Derby winner, Cicero, a somewhat fractious third. Pretty Polly and Bachelor's Button coasted along behind the others. Galloping strongly, St. Denis continued to lead as they ran down toward Swinley Bottom and then around the right-hand turn. There was now a little under a mile to go, all uphill. Six furlongs from the finish, St. Denis ran out of steam and started to fade.

Achilles was now in front.

The fast clip established by St. Denis in the early stages had left Cicero fatigued, and he too could not keep up. Pretty Polly and Bachelor's Button, running almost in tandem, began closing in on Achilles, Pretty Polly closest to the stands, with Bachelor's Button on the far side.

As if suddenly struck by exhaustion, Achilles veered towards the stands. Pretty Polly drifted out and into the lead to avoid a collision. This was the moment everyone was waiting for. The thrill of witnessing Pretty Polly's finest hour, an experience, they would tell and retell for years to come.

But Bachelor Button's jockey, Danny Maher, was not about to give over the glory. He relentlessly drove Bachelor's Button to the wire. Realizing that Bachelor's Button wasn't quitting, Pretty Polly's jockey, Bernard Dillon, went to his whip. It was the first time Pretty Polly had felt the sting of a whip. If anything, she slowed up. She was, no doubt, too exhausted to react.

Bachelor's Button won the Ascot Gold Cup by about a length over Pretty Polly. The huge gathering was devastated. A stunned silence hung over the racecourse. When Bachelor's Button was ridden to the winner's enclosure, there was barely a nod of congratulation. Countless grown men and women wept openly in the stands and the members' and royal enclosures.

The following day *Sporting Life* reported the tragedy: "Alas, and again Alas! Pretty Polly beaten! Lamentations as sincere as they were loud were heard on every hand after the race was over."

George Lambton, trainer of Lord and Lady Derby's horses, publically castigated Pretty Polly's jockey, Bernard Dillon, charging that he was at the root of the catastrophe. "If a real good jockey had been on Pretty Polly I think she might just have scrambled home."

Pretty Polly's trainer, Peter Purcell Gilpin, also blamed the jockey, claiming that he had not ridden the mare as instructed. Perhaps, to offset the fact he had hired the jockey, he added: "No doubt he was carried away by the excitement."

In the weeks and months following the race, people speculated on what had happened to Pretty Polly. The Ascot Gold Cup had been run on a hot, humid day, not conducive to a long-distance race. Furthermore, prior to the race she had be essentially mobbed by a huge crowd of fans. And then there was the fungal growth on her girth. Could that have been bothering her?

Possibly it was all these things. Although Pretty Polly was kept in training, with her owners' sights set on the Doncaster Cup, the Ascot Gold Cup would be her final race. Apparently during training Pretty Polly experienced a set-back and was retired.

Pretty Polly's fans lamented the loss. Not only would they never again enjoy the thrill of watching her glide to victory, but they would probably never see her likes again.

Pretty Polly was bold and beautiful, winning twenty-two of her twenty-four starts, without turning a hair.

Still, the odds are against even a highly exceptional racemare becoming a broodmare of great importance.

"Famous racing mares are frequently poor producers for the very reasons which made them famous: they have expended so much of their nervous energy in their races that they have little left to pass on to their progeny," wrote Federico Tesio in *Breeding the Racehorse*. First published in 1958, the book continues to be studied in the 21st century by Thoroughbred scholars.

"A large number of horses conventionally qualified as big distance runners come from mares who either have never raced at all, or have raced seldom or only over short distances. These mares were thus able to conserve—and therefore accumulate—their nervous energy."

Horses, and specifically Thoroughbreds, were Tesio's lifetime passion, bordering on obsession. His study ranged from attempting to understand the intelligence of horses to the fundamentals of breeding. As three of the world's most significant sires—Nearco, Ribot and Donatello were born of his fascination with Thoroughbreds, it is safe to assume that many of his ideas were sound.

His theory on the importance of nervous energy in breeding Thoroughbreds was born of his contemplation of genetics and the work of Austrian botanist, Gregor Johann Mendel.

Tesio was introduced to the work of Gregor Mendel on a train bound from Pisa to Rome. The man sitting directly across from Tesio, whom he described as a "foreigner," was absorbed in an "unimpressive looking booklet." When this "foreigner" stepped out of the compartment, leaving the booklet on his seat, Tesio's curiosity got the better of him. He picked up the booklet, entitled *Mendelism*, an English translation of Mendel's original German document, which traced his experiments crossing pure breeds and the ensuing hybrids.

When the book's owner returned to the compartment, he discovered his book in the hands of his travelling companion. Tesio was mesmerized by Mendel's findings, and the owner of the book allowed Tesio to continue reading. By the time Tesio had reached his destination, he had "devoured and digested it" and was contemplating how all this pertained to that most fascinating of hybrids, the Thoroughbred.

He wrote: "Mendel had experimented with two varieties of peas, a tall and a dwarf variety. Crossing the tall peas with the dwarfs he had obtained hybrids. These hybrids were not medium sized, as one might have expected, but tall. These tall hybrids, in turn, when crossed with each other, had produced tall plants and dwarfs in the proportion of three tall ones to one dwarf. In other words, nature had a tendency to return the breeds to their original pure state... it was a revelation. I had finally understood why two Thoroughbred horses, although born of the same sire and dam, in other words, full brothers (or sisters) may turn out to be the one a chestnut and a great runner, the other a bay and a mediocre performer, although both are equally well built and without apparent faults.

"The reason is that the horse which in Italy we call "purosangue" is anything but 'pure-blooded.' He is, in fact, a hybrid and as a hybrid he (or she) must follow the law of Mendel."

Tesio, however, found two traits to be common to all Thoroughbreds: "... a high degree of nervous energy and a certain 'quality' derived from selection (selective Thoroughbred breeding). The fact that these two characteristics appear in all Thoroughbreds indicates that they are not inherited according to the law of Mendel, but are passed directly from parents to offspring."

Tesio believed that stallions and mares that had long and strenuous careers on the racetrack used up much of their vitality, or nervous energy. If they were to become breeding stock, such horses would need time and rest to restore the reserve, in order to pass their vitality to their progeny.

He also concluded that mares whose racing life was arduous gave birth to offspring that "are frequently handsome, well-developed individuals without visible flaws, but they seldom win races and are beaten by others less perfect in conformation, because they have inherited a weak dose of nervous energy from a depleted parent. These offspring, by running more slowly, will not wear themselves out and may build up a new charge of energy to pass on to their own progeny."

Lady Angela's great-great grandmother, Pretty Polly, was six years old when she was sent to stud and gave birth to ten foals. None of her six sons was notable. This, would not have surprised Tesio.

Pretty Polly's four fillies, however, may have given Tesio cause to ponder. All four were not only winners, but each established her own successful family line. Lady Angela's connection was through the powerful Molly Desmond branch, a distinction she shared with the great British champion, Brigadier Gerard.

It is hard to imagine a Thoroughbred mare with a more dynamic bloodline than that of Lady Angela. The female line of both her dam and sire couldn't get much better.

Lady Angela's paternal grandam, Selene, was a top-class racehorse and exceptional matriarch. While not as outstanding as Pretty Polly on the racecourse, Selene was one of, if not *the* most notable matriarch of all time. Foaled in 1919 at Lord and Lady Derby's Stanley House outside Newmarket, England, Selene was born of the revival of the Derby family interest in horse racing.

The interest began in the late-1700s with the 12th Earl of Derby, described as a sporting young man keen on racing and even more enthusiastic about cock fighting. During the Epsom race meets, Lord Derby would invite crowds of friends to The Oaks, a converted inn near Epsom belonging to his uncle.

By all accounts, English horse racing at the time was little more than an excuse for parties and gambling. Much of the colour and spirit of the time was chronicled in the diaries and letters of Lady Sarah Lennox, the fourth daughter of the 2nd Duke of Richmond.

"Newmarket," wrote Lady Sarah in 1763, "was charming, all the charming men were there."

Referring to a private meet at a nearby estate, Lady Sarah continued, "the race at Euston was the prettiest thing I ever saw; I doated upon it, for I rid my beautiful Weazle, who was gentle enough to let me gallop backwards and forwards, so I saw the whole course."

Epsom, some fifteen miles from the centre of London, was a particularly popular venue. Initially, the crowds came to enjoy the mineral springs discovered by accident in 1618, when a farmer noticed his cows refused to drink from a particular puddle. Human consumption of the water instantly revealed its laxative qualities, and soon the mineral salts of Epsom were being marketed throughout Europe. Great crowds journeyed from London to partake of the waters at the source.

Today Epsom is home to Britain's most prominent horse race, but in the 18th century, the parties, mineral waters and gaming houses of Epsom were far more compelling than the horses. Local entrepreneurs simply added horse racing as entertainment for visitors to the spa. The races were conducted over the fine lush turf of Banstead Downs, which, according to Horace Walpole, were "covered with grass much finer than Persian carpets, and perfumed with wild thyme and juniper."

The races were generally heats of two or four miles. One summer evening in 1778, during a party at The Oaks, Lord Derby and his cronies devised a new event: a mile-and-a-half race restricted to three-year-old fillies. The race was named The Oaks, after the site of their inspiration.

The following May, Lord Derby and his friends congregated for The Oaks and fittingly, Lord Derby's filly, Bridget, won the inaugural race. While celebrating the success of The Oaks, Lord Derby and his friends decided to create a new horse-racing event. They decided to hold the race the following year; it would be open to both three-year-old fillies and colts. The distance was to be a mile, a surprisingly short race at the time. (It changed to a mile and a half in 1784.) All they needed was a name for their race.

One of Lord Derby's house guests was Sir Charles Bunbury, the son of the rector of Mildenhall. In 1762, Bunbury married Lady Sarah Lennox. It seemed an appropriate match. Bunbury lived for the turf and Lady Sarah was not only an enthusiastic and accomplished horsewoman, she was a great granddaughter of Charles II, the royal patron of Thoroughbred sport.

Lady Sarah's grandfather, Charles Lennox, born in 1672, was the illegitimate son of Charles II and his mistress, Louise de Keroualle. Louise had been appointed official mistress in 1671, but was one of many mistresses, and Charles Lennox was one of many illegitimate children of the Merry Monarch. Charles Lennox was given the title, Duke of Richmond by his Royal father, along with an estate that included a percentage of the profits from the coal mined at Newcastle.

The year after Sir Charles Bunbury and Lady Sarah were married, Bunbury was appointed Steward of the Jockey Club. Charles II was the first to attempt to create rules and order in Thoroughbred sport, and Bunbury took up the challenge with even greater zeal. By the turn of the century, Bunbury was established as Perpetual President of the Jockey Club. According to Roger Longrigg in the *History of Horse Racing*: "His single-mindedness, rectitude and courage gave the Jockey Club a moral authority which in the 19th century it sometimes conspicuously lacked."

Bunbury raced a number of exceptional horses, including the very popular Gimcrack. Barely reaching 14 hands, Gimcrack harkened back to the Scottish Galloway "running horses." A very dark grey, Gimcrack raced almost 40 times and won nearly 30, but he is remembered as the first racehorse to generate great public affection.

"There was a meeting of two days this time of year, to see the sweetest little horse run that ever was," writes Lady Sarah. "His name is Gimcrack, he is delightful."

The best horse to be bred at Bunbury's Barton Stud was Highflyer, a superb racehorse and an outstanding stallion. Bunbury sold Highflyer as a yearling to Lord Bolingbroke, of whom Lady Sarah wrote: "Bolingbroke is much the same as mad when he is drunk, and that he is generally."

After Highflyer's triumphant racing career, Bolingbroke sold the colt to Richard Tattersall. The son of a North Country farmer, Tattersall created the world's first and most important company of bloodstock auctioneers. Tattersall loved Highflyer and when the horse died in 1793, Tattersall inscribed on his tombstone: "Here lieth the perfect and beautiful symmetry of the much lamented Highflyer, by whom and his wonderful offspring the celebrated Tattersall acquired a noble fortune, but was not ashamed to acknowledge it."

Bunbury's great preoccupation with all matters regarding Thoroughbred sport gained him power and prestige within the horse-racing community, but lost him Lady Sarah. Bunbury was not interested in the arts, travel, or politics—even though he was a Member of Parliament. He lived for horses and horse racing. By the time of Derby's party to celebrate the first running of The Oaks, Bunbury was once more a bachelor: "the beautiful Lady Sarah had run off with Lord William Gordon," writes Longrigg. "The husband she left behind was rich, respectable, hypochondriac." (Of Bunbury, wrote Lady Sarah: "he loves to be thought ill.")

According to legend, in order to settle upon a name for their new one-mile horse race, Derby and Bunbury tossed a gold sovereign. But for a flip of a coin, the world's most distinguished horse race might have been called the Epsom Bunbury. In 1780, the colt Diomed, owned by Sir Charles Bunbury won the inaugural English Derby at Epsom.

When Diomed was twenty, an advanced age for a stallion, Bunbury sold him and he was shipped to the United States. Despite the enormous upheaval in the stallion's life, and the trauma of ocean voyages in the 1700s, Diomed remained virile and breeding until he was thirty. A great number of celebrated Thoroughbreds, including Lexington, considered to be one of the greatest U.S. Thoroughbreds, descend from Diomed.

The 12th Earl of Derby finally won the race that bears his name in 1787. His horse was a sturdy brown colt with the curious name of Sir Peter Teazle. Lord Derby named the colt after a character in *School For Scandal*, a comedy in which Lord Derby's future second wife, the well-known actress Elizabeth Farren played the role of Lady Teazle. Sir Peter Teazle, the horse, went on to be a leading sire. Twelve of his offspring were classic winners.

During the ensuing hundred years, the Stanley family, inheritors of the Derby title, largely abandoned their involvement in horse racing. Then in 1893 the 17th Earl of Derby decided to revive both the tradition and the famous Derby black and white racing silks. The following year Lord Derby purchased Sefton Stud, upon the death of its owner, the formidable red-haired Duchess of Montrose.

One of the grand personalities of Newmarket, the Duchess of Montrose, who raced her horses under the name Mr. Manton, had developed a very prosperous racing and breeding operation. The Duchess was known for her caustic temper, her colourful attire and her eye for a good horse And a good rider, for that matter. It was widely rumoured that the Duchess enjoyed a "passionate attachment" with Fred Archer, foremost British jockey of the 19th century.

After Lord Derby purchased Sefton Stud he changed the name to Stanley House Stud. He continued to employ the Duchess's staff, but her horses were auctioned at the 1894 Newmarket Sales. Lord Derby attended the sale with John Griffiths, who had been stud groom to the Duchess of Montrose. Upon the advice of Griffiths, Lord Derby purchased a small chestnut yearling filly, by Tristan from the mare Pilgrimage, who had won the 1878 classic double at Newmarket, the One Thousand Guineas and Two Thousand Guineas.

According to Edward John, 18th Earl of Derby in *Hyperion*, Griffiths thought the filly to be perfect, and advised his son, Walter, who would inherit his position as stud groom to the Derby stables, "Take a good look at her. Get the picture of her in your mind as a pattern all your life, and you won't go far wrong."

Lord and Lady Derby named the filly Canterbury Pilgrim and the petite, but perfectly symmetrical filly gave her new owners their first classic victory, the 1896 English Oaks.

Canterbury Pilgrim bore ten live foals, including Swynford, winner of the 1910 St. Leger and leading sire, and Chaucer. Small but durable, Chaucer raced through to his six-year-old season. He won eight races and was leading broodmare sire in 1927 and 1933. His most notable daughter was Selene.

Selene's ancestry can be traced back to the very beginnings of the Thoroughbred, to Old Bald Peg, the senior mare entered in Volume 1 of the *General Stud Book*. Published in 1793, the *General Stud Book* was James Weatherby's attempt to chronicle the breeding records of the Thoroughbred.

Old Bald Peg was foaled at the Duke of Buckingham's stud farm at Helmsley in North Yorkshire during the reign of Charles I. Her sire was recorded as an Unknown Arabian and her dam as a Barb Mare, the assumption being that the unnamed Barb mare was of imported, not of native stock.

The most popular native breed of "running horses" prior to the mid-17th century, was the now extinct Scottish Galloway. These sturdy, swift ponies were sure-footed, spirited and seldom grew taller than fourteen hands. The Scottish Galloway was employed extensively for riding, drawing carriages and racing throughout Southern Scotland and Yorkshire in Northern England.

Other horses used for racing were of Eastern, Italian and Spanish origin, and had been intermingled with the native breeds in a hodgepodge mixture of "running horse."

Thoroughbred sport as we know it today began with the ascension of Charles II, who was a particularly enthusiastic supporter of the race meets at Newmarket. To arrive in Newmarket for the 1669 Spring meeting, Charles II and his Royal party started out by coach from London at three in the morning. Under orders to arrive on time for the first race, the coachman pressed the team to its limit. As it rounded a sharp corner of the dusty dirt road, the coach tipped on its side and was dragged before the driver could rein in his frightened horses. The King and his party emerged from the overturned carriage unscathed apart from a few bruises and a thick covering of dust and dirt. They pushed the carriage back on to its wheels and continued on to Newmarket in time for the opening meet.

Charles II was highly visible at Newmarket. He could be found riding in a race, surveying the gallops from his pavilion at the top of the hill, or hacking around on Old Rowley, his trusted riding horse. (The eight-furlong Rowley Mile, site of the British classics, the One Thousand and Two Thousand, derives its name from the King's mount.)

In the summer of 1669 the Duke of Tuscany visited Newmarket Heath and was awed by the spectacle of a match race: two horses were led out "by men who were to ride them, dressed in taffeta of different colours." The horses started slowly, but "the farther they advanced in the course, the more they urged them, forcing them to continue it at full speed."

Charles II and his friends were watching on horseback and, as the two horses galloped toward the finish, the King and retinue joined in, riding flat out alongside the racers to the finish. "Trumpets and drums, which were in readiness for the purpose, sounded in applause of the conqueror." Afterwards, "His Majesty, being very much heated, adjourned to his house."

Charles II, an accomplished rider, must also have been quite physically fit, for he frequently rode his own horses in races conducted over three heats. He also quite enjoyed dancing and partying long into the night.

In 1671, English diarist, John Evelyn, described Newmarket's post-race festivities: "I found the jolly blades racing, dancing, feasting, and reveling, more resembling a luxurious rout, than a Christian Court." The Newmarket race meeting and parties lasted a fortnight. (It was during this meet that Charles II first bedded Louise de Keroualle.)

In the midst of all this cavorting, the racing world was inching toward the establishment of the Thoroughbred. Royal horse breeding was conducted on a small scale, but Charles II commissioned his Master of the Horse to procure the finest bloodlines annually in order to improve the quality of their running horses.

In order to produce a faster, more streamlined animal, the favoured bloodline to introduce into Great Britain's sturdy native breeds was the Arabian. Also known as the "desert horse," the ancestry of this breed goes back some four thousand years.

Muslim conquests initiated by the Prophet Muhammad in the 7th century proved the catalyst for the spreading of Arabian bloodlines. When Mohammed died in 632 AD, the Muslim empire extended from China to Europe. The reputation of the fast, fiery and resilient Arab horses spread with it.

In the 17th century, however, the Bedouin owners were reluctant to sell their valuable breeding horses, so British horse breeders also imported similar breeds: the Turkmene, a hotblood closely resembling the Arabian; and the Barb. Originally from Morocco, the Barb is also a horse of the desert and, like the Arabian horse, known for stamina and endurance. There the resemblance begins and ends.

The Arabian horse has a unique skeletal conformation. All other breeds have eighteen ribs, six lumbar bones, and eighteen tail vertebrae. The Arabian has one less rib, one less lumbar bone, and two fewer tail vertebrae, which accounts for their high tail carriage. Other distinctive characteristics include a conspicuously dished face, large widely-spaced eyes, a fairly straight shoulder, flat knees and short canon bones.

The Barb, on the other hand, is not a pretty horse. One theory holds that the Barb evolved from wild horses that escaped the Ice Age. The narrow skull formation of the Barb certainly resembles that of the primitive horse. The face of the Barb is either straight or Roman-nosed. Its tail is set low, and it is a taller and bigger horse than the Arabian. Still, the Barb was the horse of the hard-riding Berber, who were instrumental in the Muslim Conquest.

Admiral Henry Rous, the self-proclaimed horse-racing authority of Great Britain in the mid-19th century wrote a treatise entitled *On the Laws and Practice of Horse Racing*. In the preface he proclaims:

"The English racehorse boasts of a pure descent from the Arabian, and under whatever denomination the original stock of our Thoroughbred horses have been imported ... they were true sons and daughters of the desert."

However well-meaning, his assertion is decidedly flawed. The conformation, temperament, size and scope of the Thoroughbred are very different from those of the Arabian. The Thoroughbred is, in fact, of mixed origin whose precise combination is lost.

This hybrid horse is quite extraordinary. It combines the Arabian, a horse able to endure extreme heat, designed to carry its Bedouin rider across endless desert sands, with the Galloway, a horse able to endure the damp and cold weather of Scotland, race through bogs and over hill and dale.

It is agreed, however, that all modern Thoroughbreds trace their male-line ancestry to three stallions: the Byerley Turk, the Darley Arabian, and the Godolphin Arabian.

The Byerley Turk, a brown colt believed to have been foaled in 1684, was seized from a Turkish Army officer at Buda in 1687 by Captain Byerley of County Durham, who apparently rode the horse at the Battle of the Boyne in 1690.

The Darley Arabian, a bay colt foaled in 1700, was sent to England as a gift for John Darley of Yorkshire from his brother, a merchant living in Syria. The Darley Arabian was four when he arrived in England and both his dam and sire were of the pure Arabian strain of Managhi.

The Godolphin Arabian, a bay colt, was foaled in 1724 in Yemen. He was sold to Syrian interests, then to the Bey of Tunis, who in turn, gave the colt to the King of France who sold him to Edward Coke, of Derbyshire. When Coke died in 1733, he bequeathed all his horses, including this well-travelled Arabian stallion, to a London Bloodstock agent, who sold him to the second Earl of Godolphin. The Godolphin Arabian stood at Gog Magog, near Newmarket, until his death in 1753. (His constant companion was a scruffy orange cat called Grimalkin. When Grimalkin died, the Godolphin Arabian became distraught; thereafter he detested all cats and attempted to savage any that came close to him.) The Godolphin Arabian was buried beneath the Gog Magog stable gateway.

As Tony Morris wrote in *Thoroughbred Stallions*: "There can be no denying that all three horses were important stallions in their day...It was essentially the crossing of the imported stallions from the east with the English native-bred mares which produced the Thoroughbred. Both made vital contributions; the one could not have done it without the other. The much glorified "great triumvirate" were not the only successful imported sires of their era, and the fact that their male-line descendants flourished more obviously than those of some others does not mean that those whose female descendants excelled were not equally, perhaps ever more, significant."

The General Stud Book lists 103 imported stallions. Other sources indicated there were more like 160. *The General Stud Book* lists 78 tap-root mares (mares whose female progeny have prospered); other sources suggest the number is more like 50.

Accuracy is impossible, because many horses had various names. When they changed ownership they changed apparent identity. According to whim, or commercial advantage, the horses also changed breed, alternating between Barb, Turk and Arab. Against this, many horses shared names. Dimple, Cricket, Why Not, Merlin, Careless, Bonny Black—some of the most resounding names are the same for both father and son. Mothers and daughters, too were often called by the same name.

Imported horses were given names suggesting their country of origin, but these too, were often erroneous: the breed assigned to imported horses was not always accurate, for example if a horse was purchased in Turkey it would be called a Turk, even if it was an Arabian. To further confuse things, the British frequently referred to all horses imported from the south as Arabians.

When it comes to the female lines, there is even more confusion. For example, there are a number of Barb mares in the stud book. But the name Howard Barb mare does not necessarily mean that the mare belonged to Howard, more likely she was a daughter of the Howard Barb. The number of Royal Mares is unknown because most of the mares belonging to the King were described as a Royal Mare. And then there are mares with confusing designations like Dam of Clubfoot Daughter of Hautboy.

The first clearly exceptional Thoroughbred was called Flying Childers. Bred by Mr. Leonard Childers of Doncaster, the horse was foaled in 1715 and sold to the Duke of Devonshire. By all accounts Flying Childers was so perfect that he was considered an unrepeatable phenomenon.

In many ways Flying Childers embodied the vision of a magnificent British Thoroughbred. His brother, Bartlett's Childers, did not race because he suffered from weak blood vessels, but because of the prominence of Flying Childers, he stood at stud and is remembered as the great-grandsire of Britain's second outstanding racehorse, Eclipse.

There is some debate over the actual ancestry of the two Childers horses. The *General Stud Book* indicates that their sire was the Darley Arabian and their dam was Betty Leedes by Old Careless. One thing is for certain: several generations back, on both sides of the family tree, we find the original matriarch, Old Bald Peg.

"Breeding champions can take a long time, and requires endless patience. The music goes round and round, and it's lucky if it comes out at all. On the other hand, it is of profound satisfaction to have been the owner of the great granddam, and the breeder of the granddam and the dam of a horse like Mill Reef."

PAUL MELLON

At some point, the equine chain that traced back to Old Bald Peg had disappeared from England. In the mid-19ᵗʰ century, William Blenkiron, set out to correct this situation. Eventually he discovered Old Bald Peg descendants quartered in France. In 1869, Blenkiron bought the mare Fenella, as a yearling, from a French count. Eight years later he abandoned his breeding project, declaring Fenella to be "of no account" and sold her to an Austrian horse breeder.

Less than a year after Blenkiron banished Fenella, her daughter began making a name on Britain's racecourses. The filly was Douranee, purchased as a yearling by Hugh Lupus Grosvenor. Reputed to be the wealthiest person in England, Grosvenor had recently obtained the title of Duke of Westminster, and was spending an unprecedented sum to build up his stud, Eaton Hall in Cheshire.

Douranee won eleven races for the Duke of Westminster, so he dispatched an agent to Austria in search of her dam, Fenella. He bought Fenella and brought her back to Eaton Hall. Before long, according to *Hyperion*, the Duke got bored with the project: "he also tired of Douranee, selling her, together with Ormonde, to a Buenos Aires buyer in 1889, for shipment to Argentina."

If, in the inexact science of horse breeding, great patience is rewarded, is lack of patience, penalized? The Duke of Westminster certainly was. Furthermore, selling Ormonde made him extremely unpopular.

Ormonde was hugely well-liked among British racing fans. Backward and gangly as a youngster, Ormonde grew into a magnificent 16-hand horse with a deep chocolate-coloured coat and the heart of a lion. By the end of his three-year-old season, he was undefeated in 11 races and one walk-over (no one would go against him). His victories including the 1886 Triple Crown (Two Thousand Guineas, The Derby and St. Leger). To celebrate Queen Victoria's Jubilee that year, the Duke of Westminster hosted a party for members of British, European, and Asian royal families. The centre of attention was Ormonde. People brought him all manner of gift, including orchids and carnations, which, to the delight of his fans, he proceeded to eat.

The following year Ormonde was sent to the post four times (including another walk-over), and was made to carry as much as 136 pounds. (In one race Ormonde carried 25 pounds more than his nearest rival.) Ormonde was never defeated, however he had contracted a breathing problem.

The Duke of Westminster retired Ormonde to stud at his Eaton Hall. The next year the Duke leased Ormonde to Lord Gerard at Newmarket. Ormonde caught a chill and was so ill that he was unable to perform his stallion duties, so Lord Gerard sent the horse back to the Duke, who sold Ormonde to the Argentine horse dealer. Ormonde and his travelling companion, Douranee, were shipped to Argentina. The dealer then sold Ormonde to a California breeder and Ormonde was back at sea. Douranee remained in Argentina.

Ormonde's progeny were not many — his fertility had been severely affected by his illness at Newmarket. The long and, no doubt, harrowing voyages by land and sea also must have played havoc with Ormonde's precarious health. Still, Ormonde's offspring were of good quality. From Ormonde's first crop came Orme, the very fine racehorse and sire, who gave Westminster his second Triple Crown winner, Flying Fox, from his second crop of yearlings.

The Duke, incidentally, did not intend the breeding that resulted in Flying Fox. He had purchased Vampire, the dam of Flying Fox, and planned to send her to a fashionable stallion, not to the young unproven Orme, who was in residence at Eaton Hall. Vampire, however, was discovered to possess such a wicked disposition that it was thought hazardous to send her to another stud. She was therefore put to the resident stallion Orme. Following the triumph of Flying Fox, Orme and Vampire were mated many times but without appreciable success.

Ormonde and Orme are also in the family tree of Nearctic. Orme is Lady Angela's great-great-great grandfather.

There is no record of what happened to Fenella: although her daughter, Douranee, was sold to Argentina, Douranee's first foal remained in England. Named Gondola, she raced only once, as a two-year-old. She was unplaced and retired, which suggests that she was either hurt or disinclined to race.

In 1902, the three-year-old Gondola was bred to Loved One and the following spring gave birth to a filly. As a yearling the filly was sent to auction and purchased by Major Edwardes for a mere 75 guineas; Edwardes named her Gondolette. When she was two, he took her to Epsom and entered her in a selling-race, after which he sold Gondolette to Lord Westbury for 800 guineas. Lord Westbury then sold her to Lord Wavertree.

In 1912 Lord Wavertree entered Gondolette in the Newmarket December sales; she was in foal to Minoru. Walter Alston, Lord Derby's bloodstock manager, purchased Gondolette for 1,550 guineas.

Gondolette was taken to Lord Derby's Stanley House Stud, where she would bring the glory of two English Derby winners to Lord and Lady Derby.

In *Hyperion,* Walter Griffiths, Lord Derby's stud groom at Newmarket described Gondolette as "just a plain ordinary sort of mare. Her best feature was her sturdiness of limb. She had a beautiful set of legs. I remember her particularly for her unusually independent character. In the paddock she hated the company of others, and no mare dared go near her, although I never knew her to kick in all her life. She always insisted on drinking alone at the water-tank. If any other mare approached she would just look at her and sort of snarl, this was quite sufficient to ensure her being undisturbed."

The following spring, Gondolette gave birth to a bay filly, Serenissima, dam of Selene. Several months later a son of Gondolette, Great Sport, finished third in the English Derby. (Great Sport was one of three foals that Gondolette had produced prior to taking up residence at Stanley House.) The second of these foals was a filly born in 1911. Named Dolabella, she won only one race, but would become the dam of seven winners. In fact, all eight of Gondolette's daughters were the dams of winners.

Gondolette's third foal was a bay colt named Let Fly. In 1915 Let Fly finished second in the English Derby. Thus, within two years, two sons of Gondolette had finished in the frame in the English Derby. In 1918, Gondolette's daughter, Ferry, won the English classic One Thousand Guineas and was second in The Oaks.

When the 17th Earl of Derby set out to recreate the family racing stable, no horse carrying its black and white racing silks had won the race named for his ancestor since Sir Peter Teazle in 1787. It was the Earl's dream to win this great horse race.

Gondolette bore three colts: the first finished third in the Derby; the second finished second in the Derby. The third colt, the only one born at Stanley House Stud, won the Derby.

The year was 1924. Ridden by a 21-year-old Yorkshire lad,

Tommy Weston, Sansovino passed the winning post six lengths ahead of St. Germans. According to *Hyperion*, Lord Derby was ecstatic: "It was said of Sansovino's owner that day that he was 'the wettest and certainly the happiest man' on Epsom racecourse, as he walked out through the drenching rain to lead his winner into the unsaddling enclosure."

Gondolette died the following year. But her gifts to Lord and Lady Derby were far from over.

Of all of Gondolette's daughters, Serenissima was to follow Gondolette. Like her dam, Serenissima was not inspired to race; at three she won two insignificant events. Serenissima, however, gave birth to twelve foals. A daughter, Tranquil, won eight races including the One Thousand Guineas, St. Leger, and Jockey Club Gold Cup. A son, Bosworth, won the Ascot Club Gold Cup and was second in the St. Leger. But her greatest offspring was a tiny bay filly born at Stanley House Stud in the spring of 1919. Her name was Selene.

Selene was named after the Greek Goddess of the Moon, but initially, some people were unable to see anything divine in the filly. George Lambton, trainer for the Derby horses, was one of those people. Given her small stature, Lambton advised Lord and Lady Derby not to nominate Selene to England's classic horse races.

Lambton completely underestimated Selene: the petite filly sped to victory sixteen times and was never out of the money. Yet Lambton's hasty judgement disallowed her from running in England's classic races: by the time he realized that she was a great champion, the nominations were closed.

Selene's granddam, Canterbury Pilgrim, wasn't much bigger than a pony; yet she won The Oaks, the Park Hill Stakes and Jockey Club Stakes. After retiring from racing, Canterbury Pilgrim gave birth to the extremely important sires, Swynford and Chaucer, Selene's diminutive sire.

Pilgrimage, the dam of Canterbury Pilgrim and English Derby winner, Jeddah, won *both* the English One Thousand Guineas and

Two Thousand Guineas, an extremely rare event. (The One Thousand Guineas is restricted to three-year-old fillies, the Two Thousand Guineas is open to three-year-old fillies and colts.) Pilgrimage is also dam of Loved One, thus Pilgrimage is the granddam of Gondolette.

Selene was not only an outstanding racehorse, she is the matriarch to a vast international dynasty of champions. Possibly the pre-eminent broodmare in history, Selene, is the great-great-grandam to legends such as Native Dancer, Buckpasser and Kelso. In South America, many top Thoroughbreds trace their lineage back to Selene through her son, Hunter's Moon. Her most famous son, however, both as a stallion and a racehorse, is Hyperion, grandsire of Nearctic.

For some time Charlie Brown, the stud manager at Woodhay near Newbury, had been trying to convince Lord Derby's bloodstock manager, William Alston, to breed Selene with his stallion Gainsborough. Brown liked Selene's pedigree, her conformation and her spirit. He had seen her race and felt she was a perfect match for his 1917 Triple Crown winner.

Gainsborough was owned and bred by Lady Douglas who, in the early 1900s, had set up Woodhay stud. One of her first purchases was a chestnut filly she named Rosedrop, who went on to win the 1910 Oaks. In the spring of each of the next three years Rosedrop was bred to Bayardo. The first year she was barren; the second year she gave birth to a bay filly, La Tosca; and the third year she produced a bay colt, Gainsborough.

As a yearling Gainsborough was sent to the Newmarket Sales, but bidding failed to meet his reserve of 2,000 guineas. So, back to Lady Douglas he went. Gainsborough developed into a grand-looking colt. He ran in nine races and won five, including the British Triple Crown races, the Two Thousand Guineas, Derby and St. Leger.

William Alston gained Lord Derby's consent to have Selene bred with Gainsborough in 1929 and she was shipped to Newbury near the end of February. Selene, however, was not interested in the handsome bay stallion.

Alston told Charlie Brown to send Selene home; she would rest for the next twelve months and be bred to the stallion Son-in-Law the following season. Charlie Brown asked permission to bring Selene and Gainsborough together one more time. Alston grudgingly conceded.

Eleven months later, on 18 April, 1930, a blustery, damp morning, Selene lay down in her stall, ready to give birth. It was Good Friday and the staff at Lord Derby's Stanley House Stud had not experienced an Easter so wintry for years.

Selene was now eleven and this was her fifth foal. Her first two foals were brown colts. The second two, bay colts. Both Selene and Gainsborough were bay with black points. So when Selene's new foal poked out a tiny white hoof, followed by a tiny white sock capping its tiny auburn leg, the foaling crew were a bit surprised. Soon the foal was lying on the straw next to Selene. His damp coat was light-red chestnut with four white socks, and he was so small that one of the lads joked that he looked more like a golden retriever than a horse.

Yet, on this cold gloomy day, when Lady Derby saw this little foal's radiant coat, she immediately decided to name him Hyperion for the father of Helios, god of the sun.

In September 1930 Hyperion was weaned from Selene and he joined the other youngsters in a spacious paddock. Not far from the gate there was an overhead shelter in the style of a run-in shed, beneath which was a feeding trough. There was plenty of room for the weanlings, Hyperion, however, appeared bothered by the height of the trough. So he tried snatching mouthfuls of hay from the lower part, which required him to splay his forelegs, thus making him a vulnerable target for the bigger colts.

Finally they moved Hyperion and another small colt, to a different location. Harry Peachey was given responsibility for the little colts:

"It would be October-November time," recalled Peachey in *Hyperion*, "and d'you know Hyperion was so tiny, he couldn't reach up properly to take his fodder from the ordinary foal manger, and we had to have a three-foot-high wooden job specially made up for him, so he could eat in comfort."

The following spring Peachey observed Hyperion's unusual

interest in the kestrels and sparrow-hawks hovering high above his paddock: "As soon as one swooped into the hedge-row, the little horse would go galloping there, full tilt, to see what had happened."

Adrian Scope, Derby's stud manager in later years, added his recollections of Hyperion's curious behaviour: "When sent away from Newmarket to Yorkshire during the war, he spent hours each day out in the paddocks watching the pheasants—and when a number had gathered together on the ground, up he would gallop and scare them away."

Federico Tesio would have enjoyed observing Hyperion. Many of his insights into the nature of the Thoroughbred were gained in his silent observation of his horses. Often he spent hours, just sitting, watching. During one of these sessions Tesio became quite curious about the eyesight of a horse.

As he wrote in *Breeding the Racehorse*, "I have browsed through many books, old ones and modern ones, in several different languages, but none of them mentions the subject. I have asked veterinarians and cavalry officers, coachmen and jockeys. They all told me that the matter had never occurred to them, so one day I resolved to find out for myself."

Tesio conducted a series of experiments, from which he observed that a Thoroughbred has difficulty distinguishing objects at a distance farther than 150 yards. He also noted that he had "never seen a horse raise his eyes to look at the sky or at the top of a tall tree or at a second storey window of a house..."

Tesio worked his horses at Ciampino, the racetrack outside Rome. There was an airport adjacent to the training tracks, yet the horses took no notice of the airplanes, even though the planes' take off frequently passed thirty or forty yards above the horses' heads.

In part this would be due to the physiology of the horse. The neck slants diagonally upward; they have limited upward movement, but considerable movement downward. Moreover, the head is almost at right angles to the neck, and points toward the ground, so that the horse may graze—which, given its druthers, a horse will do for up to 16 hours a day.

Hyperion's neck was set slightly higher than most, but that should not have had a noticeable affect on his behaviour. Five years after his death at twenty-nine, it was decided that Hyperion's skeleton be assembled for display in a museum. The job was assigned to Professor William Miller, former head of the Equine Research Station. Miller discovered an unusual thickening of the hyoid bone on the left side of Hyperion's face in the ear area indicating that Hyperion probably suffered from deafness and very possibly had done so since he was quite young.

This would explain Hyperion's curious behaviour, for no one watching Hyperion on the Newmarket Heaths would have guessed that he was destined to be a great champion. Not only was he the size of a pony, but he did not act like a normal young Thoroughbred.

In a note to Lord Derby in the spring of 1932, trainer George Lambton wrote: "The two-year-olds are backward, Hyperion particularly so." Lambton decided against travelling to Doncaster for Hyperion's first race, having little confidence in the tiny chestnut colt.

His rider didn't have much faith in Hyperion either. After several training gallops over Newmarket heath, Tommy Weston opined that Hyperion was either "dead lazy, or next to useless."

While the other young horses snorted and kicked up their heels as they scampered over the lush turf, Hyperion seemed content to amble along. He was in no way affected by the antics of the others. He also had the habit of coming to a complete halt whenever and wherever the notion struck him.

This is likely due to his hearing impairment. Horses have amazing hearing. Their ears are extremely sensitive and they can distinguish a far more extensive range of sound than their human companions. Where humans, in their prime, detect sound at approximately 20,000 cycles per second, horses can hear up to 25,000 cycles per second. Each ear operates independently and can rotate about 180 degrees. This allows the horse to hone in on a particular noise emanating from a great distance. This highly-developed hearing harkens back to the fact that the horse is a flight animal. Predators have padded feet, and stealth. To survive, the horse must be able to detect the slightest squeak.

An inability to perceive sounds accurately at a distance would explain why Hyperion would stop to peruse the countryside while the rest of the pack galloped on. It explained why Hyperion acted nonchalant on the quiet heath, but became supercharged in the extremely noisy environment of a racetrack.

When Hyperion made his racing debut at two, he was a mere fourteen hand two inches (four foot, two inches), the size of a child's pony. The location was Doncaster, the date 27 May 1932: the day the other side of Hyperion's personality revealed itself.

Rain drizzled on the heavy turf on this grey, overcast afternoon. Lambton, Hyperion's trainer, sent jockey Tommy Weston with the instructions: "Don't use the whip on him, but don't finish last."

When Weston walked out of the jockeys weighing-room, he was surprised to see Hyperion bouncing around the parade ring, uncharacteristically animated, alert to the crowds, the excitement, and general racecourse clamour. Hyperion's lad, Tom Theobald, gave Weston a leg-up on to Hyperion, then detached the lead rein, shook his head and said: "You wouldn't think he's the same horse as the one we know back home."

For many young horses, coming from the tranquil countryside to the frenetic energy of the racecourse for the first time, can be quite unnerving. Not so Hyperion. He cantered down to the start, his ears perked, his eyes bright and inquisitive. The pandemonium may have allowed Hyperion to discern sounds clearly for the first time.

The Zetland Plate had attracted a field of nineteen. The bookmakers lumped Hyperion in with a dozen "others" at 25 — 1 odds. Halfway down the straight Weston tapped Hyperion on the shoulder with his whip, just to ensure that they didn't finish last. Hyperion bounded forward so quickly Weston had to scramble to stay in the saddle, and finished a fast-closing fourth. Later Weston confided that had he known that Hyperion was a racehorse, he would have ridden him differently: "Run the race again, he would win by two or three lengths."

Two weeks later Hyperion confirmed Weston's praise. The event was the five-furlong New Stakes at Ascot. Twenty-two horses went to the post with the superior filly, Nun's Veil, firmly favoured at 6-4. Her trainer, Fred Darling, was so confident that en route to the saddling boxes he asked a friend to place a large bet with the bookmakers on his behalf.

Fred Darling's hopes of a big win were dashed by one very small, gold-coloured colt. The starter's pistol cracked, and twenty-two young horses began their charge. Hyperion shot to the front of the pack, like a stag outdistancing the hounds, and won the sprint by three lengths in a blistering 61 seconds.

Great things were now expected of the little golden colt. Yet, when Hyperion returned to Newmarket, he reverted to his nonchalant self, uninterested in training, he continued to prefer ambling to galloping.

The consensus was that Hyperion had grown lazier since his two-year-old days, and occasionally his rider was equipped with dull spurs, to persuade Hyperion to put forth some effort. As Hyperion looked less and less like a Derby winner, it appeared likely that his trainer and his jockey would be dismissed by Lord Derby. George Lambton was in poor health, and Lord Derby had the notion that Tommy Weston had either lost his nerve or was pulling Derby's horses. The team did, however, remain together for the season.

Had it not been for his misjudging Selene because of her size, George Lambton might well have made the same mistake with Hyperion. Instead, even though Hyperion looked like a small, but perfect pony and was not inclined to race, Lambton posted his nomination fees to England's classic horse races.

However, Hyperion was not entered in the Two Thousand Guineas, the first of England's Triple Crown races. Instead, Hyperion made his three-year-old debut a week later, 2 May 1933, in the Chester Vase, a mile-and-a-half allowance race for three-and four-year-olds. There were eleven starters and Hyperion received a ten-pound allowance. Prior to the race, Lambton was non-committal: "He's so idle that I don't quite know what to make of him, but I'm pleased with his progress."

There had been heavy rain and Hyperion galloped along the spongy turf course without any sense of urgency until he was challenged by an Irish outsider, Franz Hals. Tommy Weston tapped Hyperion's right shoulder with his crop and the colt soared across the finish, first by two lengths. This was Hyperion's only racecourse appearance prior to the English Derby on 31 May.

British racing fans loved Hyperion. In the few minutes it takes for the horses to canter up the track and past the stands to the start of the Derby, the crowd had made him the 6-1 favourite. They cheered as Tommy Weston kept Hyperion tucked close to the rail, chasing his pacemaker Thrapston. They cheered as he rounded Tattenham Corner, passing Thrapston and taking the lead coming into the straightaway. The roar became deafening as the little golden colt with the four white socks distanced himself farther and farther from the field. And when Hyperion flew past the finish, close to six lengths ahead of his nearest rival the crowds went wild. (The official measurement was four lengths, but the photos show a much greater distance between Hyperion and the second horse, King Salaman.)

Hyperion's victory was one of the most popular in Derby history.

A fortnight later, Hyperion went on to win the Prince of Wales's Stakes, over one mile and five furlongs, on the first day at Royal Ascot. When Hyperion returned to Newmarket, he was lame in his hindquarters due to a slight dislocation of his stifle joint. By the fall, however, Hyperion was once again sound and ready to contest the lengthy (mile-and-six 3/5 furlongs) St. Leger Stakes at Doncaster. Even though Hyperion had not raced over the summer, his popularity continued to grow. When he joined the field of 14 for the St. Leger, a large crowd turned out to cheer for their diminutive champion.

Tommy Weston allowed Hyperion to canter along in front of the pack. Several horses chased up after him, but each time Weston simply gave Hyperion a bit more rein. And each time, Hyperion's fans hollered. And they continued to holler as Hyperion coasted to a three-length victory.

At the end of the year, Lord Derby decided it was time for George Lambton to retire "and give way to a younger man." Lambton had been training horses for Derby since 1893, but now their long and prosperous relationship turned sour. Lambton continued training for other clients and Colledge Leader took over training Derby's of racehorses, including Hyperion.

Leader did not appear to understand Hyperion and did not bring him to the races physically fit. Hyperion won his first four-year-old race at Newmarket by a mere neck, and the second, a fortnight later, by less than a length.

A month later things really started falling apart. Tommy Weston, a generally cheerful Yorkshireman, was unhappy with Hyperion's new trainer. Prior to the Ascot Gold Cup he was gloomy and apprehensive and told a reporter "I wish he weren't running—not me riding him." By all accounts Hyperion was not fit, and he finished third, eight lengths behind the leader. Tommy Weston openly blamed the trainer; Leader, in turn, insisted that Weston's contract be terminated, which it was, at the end of the season.

In the midst of all this discord it was decided to race Hyperion again. It was a stupid decision, made worse by the fact that only one other horse showed up to race and Hyperion was made to carry 29 pounds more than the other horse. Still Hyperion lost this encounter only by the narrowest margin. Before any further damage could be done, Hyperion was retired.

Hyperion was the leading stallion in Great Britain in six different years, and twice the leading sire of broodmares. Hydroplane II, dam of U.S. Triple Crown winner, Citation, may have been his most celebrated daughter, Lady Angela was certainly his most important daughter.

Among horses, Nearco was a god. Born of another time, Zeus surely would have invited Nearco to roam Mount Olympus. Perhaps Nearco was the incarnation of Pegasus, for he surely was courageous, seemingly invincible—and, he could fly.

The tale of Nearco began in England on a cold damp afternoon at the December 1915 Newmarket sales. The auctioneer was trying to sell a mournful, light-boned filly by the name of Catnip; she had made ten starts, with only one win, in a modest event over the remote Newcastle course. Catnip was, however, beautifully bred. She was a daughter of One Thousand Guineas winner, Sibola, and by English Derby winner, Spearmint.

Catnip's dismal race record inspired little interest among the buyers that day—except for Federico Tesio. He purchased Catnip for a mere 75 guineas and was said to have been chuckling to himself as he left the sales ring to acquaint himself with his new mare. As Patrick Robinson notes in *Classic Lines,* Tesio's jubilation "prompted some members of the British racing establishment to remark that 'he was not only foreign, but quite possibly mad.'"

Tesio was convinced that Catnip was precisely what he needed in order to fulfil his long-term goal—of creating the supreme Thoroughbred athlete.

Of Catnip's brood of foals, the most significant racehorse and, subsequently, broodmare, was a compact, rather plain-looking dark bay filly that Tesio named Nogara. Nogara won fourteen races, including two Italian classics, before retiring to Tesio's small band of broodmares. Nearco is the proof of human folly, a reminder that the only certainty in the breeding of great Thoroughbred champions, is uncertainty. If Tesio, recognized as the breeder of Nearco, had had his way, there would not have been a Nearco.

Federico Tesio was born 17 July 1869 in Turin, Italy. As a young man he set out to see the world. His wanderings gave him insight into the nature of the horse in a wide range of environments. Yet the catalyst for his travel, according to his friend and business partner, Mario Incisa della Rochetta, in *The Tesios As I Knew Them,* was a personal matter.

"Rumour had it that the reason behind his departure on these first travels was an unsuccessful attempt on the virtue of a married woman. It happened at the Hotel Nettuno in Pisa. He had conceived the insane idea of trying to seduce the lady by entering her bedroom through the window. It seems that his ejection, by the same route, was instantaneous. Whether from anger or shame (far be it from me to suspect that it was from fear of her husband), Tesio left Pisa at dawn the following morning and set out on his journey around the world."

Tesio's adventures took him to China and Japan where he became fascinated by cultural differences between Eastern and Western societies. Of the Japanese he commented that they "have better taste than us—small houses with a few beautiful things; not these dreadful buildings of ours crammed from floor to ceiling with oddments from every epoch! And then we enter with our shoes on!" This last comment apparently did not dissuade him from walking about his own home in the same shoes he wore when touring his stables.

Tesio also journeyed to Argentina, where he rode from Buenos Aires to Patagonia, across the Pampas, with only his *tropilla*—small herd of horses—for company. When the horse he was riding grew weary, he simply chose another from his *tropilla* for on the next leg of the expedition. He described how the entire *tropilla* would lie on the ground when the *pampero*, a strong cold wind, was about to blow across the Pampas, although the air was still perfectly calm.

Tesio's Dormello Stud on the banks of Lake Maggiore in

Northern Italy was a collection of very small farms. Tesio was not a man of wealth, often struggling to make ends meet. His band of broodmares was moderate, seldom more than a dozen at a time; in sixty years he bred only about a thousand Thoroughbreds. Yet, his influence is profound and flows in the blood of today's finest racehorses.

Tesio was fastidious when selecting a mate for a mare. He was known to travel long distances solely to inspect the facilities and staff of a farm standing a stallion he was considering.

Of his broodmares, Nogara, the dam of Nearco, was one of his great favourites. Her small, compact conformation was considered ideal. When it came to deciding upon the mate for Nogara, Tesio was particularly thorough. After great and painstaking deliberation, Tesio was determined that Fairway, owned by Lord Derby, was absolutely perfect. From physique to disposition, they were complimentary.

Unfortunately Tesio's deliberations took such a long time that by the time he finally made up his mind Fairway's book was full. "Tesio was in despair," wrote Mario Incisa della Rochetta.

Instead, Tesio reluctantly shipped Nogara to France to be bred to Fairway's full brother, Pharos. Where Fairway had won the St. Leger Stakes, at almost two miles, Pharos had not shown himself to be a distance horse. Compact and muscular, Pharos was the physical opposite of Fairway. Tesio had calculated that Nogara's conformation would be complimented by a tall rangy horse. He held no hope for the outcome of the mating of Nogara and Pharos.

On 24 January 1935, nineteen years after his journey to Newmarket to purchase Catnip, Tesio watched her daughter, Nogara, give birth to Nearco. He was a small, stocky, dark bay foal. Tesio wasn't impressed. Not yet.

Wilful and strong, Nearco bullied the other foals. One of his favourite games was to trot up and plow into another colt with his shoulder, frequently sending his victim staggering. Nearco's aggressive behaviour was encouraging to Tesio: perhaps this colt might make a racehorse after all.

During his travels, Tesio had crossed the Canadian prairies, where he came upon a herd of 20,000 migrating bison. It was autumn, and he wondered how they knew when and where to go. Upon his return to Italy, he recognized that his broodmares, too, exhibited migratory behaviour. In the fall, when turned out on to a new pasture, the mares grazed across the field; when they had stripped it bare of grass they stood anxiously at the southern end of the paddock. As winter approached, the mares dug in the ground to get at the grass roots, and again they stood anxiously at the southern end of the paddock.

Tesio wondered if their instincts were telling them that it was time to migrate in order that their youngsters would benefit from continued grazing in warmer climates.

So, in the fall of 1935, the year Nearco was born, and every year thereafter, Tesio shipped his weanlings south to spend the winter grazing and growing at Olgiata, the estate of Mario Incisa della Rochetta.

Was this migration experiment successful? The only evidence is that three of Federico Tesio's greatest horses—Donatello, Ribot and Nearco—were participants in the experiment.

"Nearco's character began to assert itself after weaning when he arrived to winter at Olgiata," wrote Mario Incisa della Rochetta. "He would never leave his companions alone in the paddock... He was strong and stocky, what was known in the old Roman *campagna* as a "winner." Tesio was delighted when he saw him again. He liked the youngster's aggressiveness.

"Nearco was incredibly tough. During his training he took whatever came his way, under whatever weight he was given... It was impossible to add anything to his capabilities by extra work or to subtract anything by reducing it because he did exactly what he wanted, in the way he wanted."

Because Tesio had no income other than from his horses, he required top horses to win top-class races. He therefore subjected each of his horses to the severest tests in order to discover the very best.

"... it would be improper to suggest that Tesio was the greatest trainer that ever existed, but what I am suggesting is that Tesio's supreme moment as a creator and artist came when he sat down on his folding stick in his stable yard and studied his horses." wrote Franco Varola in *The Tesio Myth*. "Sometimes he would remain for hours on end watching their every movement and reaction. Whatever the leanings of a trainer who trains for other people, he cannot afford to spend so many hours just doing that. He is simply too busy with a number of other tasks. But the advantage of Tesio as a trainer, over everyone in this profession, was that he could afford to study his own horses. This intensive study could lead him to change distance, or to change racing plans, or to change riding tactics."

Tesio was an exacting and extremely demanding trainer, some say too tyrannical in his conditioning methods. Tesio insisted that his horses be in the absolute peak of condition when they went into a race, but no matter how severely he tested Nearco's superiority and indifference, the grand colt barely turned a hair. Nearco simply did whatever Federico Tesio asked of him. A magnificent combination of power and grace, with an unflappable disposition, Nearco was neither bad-tempered nor difficult. At the sound of the starter's pistol he simply galloped off and won with coolness and detachment to the actual event.

Nearco was powerful, resolute, mentally impervious and had brilliant speed. He won every time he stepped on to a racecourse, with disregard, if not complete disdain for the others.

On 10 June 1937 two-year-old Nearco already looked like a mature, fully developed horse when he made his first appearance on a racecourse. (He was not raced again until the fall, winning three races in September, two more in October, and one in November.) Tesio chose not to race Nearco during the summer months, presumably because he realized that there was little to be gained contesting July events, when the ground was usually hard.

Nearco's final two-year-old race, the demanding Premio Chiusura over seven furlongs straight, was particularly memorable. The photograph of the finish shows Nearco being held back and his stable-mate, El Greco, straining for all he was worth. When the two colts crossed the post, their three opponents were nowhere to be seen.

Nearco won each of his two-year-old starts with ease and at three he was even more formidable. He had developed into what many considered to be the perfect racehorse—an exquisite balance of grace and power.

There seemed to be no limit to Nearco's potential. His disposition was perfect, and he simply did whatever was required of him, whether in the morning gallops or in competition.

"Nearco was a law unto himself," wrote Varola. "Some of his races were easy to the point of dullness, due to his devastating superiority, but I still recall it as one of my greatest emotions when, after the start of the Derby Italiano, he proceeded to leave the field on the spot, gradually increasing his advantage up to the point when [his jockey] Gubellini had to restrain him in order not to waste his energies unnecessarily... Nearco was so superior that he could break away at the start and win by as much as he pleased without taking notice of his rivals."

"It was like a dream," wrote Mario Incisa della Rochetta. "There was never even the slightest hitch in his career, not even a touch of colic or a moment's lameness. Unbeaten in his two-year-old races, he went on at three to take the Premio Parioli, the Italian Derby, the Gran Premio d'Italia, the Gran Premio di Milano and, finally the Grand Prix de Paris.

Nearco won the Premio Parioli (the Italian Two Thousand

Guineas) by six lengths, and was so far out in front in the Italian Derby, that the steward simply declared Nearco's winning margin to be "a distance." His thirteenth and final race in Italy was the 1-7/8-mile Gran Premio di Milano, in which he cruised home three lengths ahead of the rest.

Tesio then decided to test his colt against the best in the world. He chose the mile-and-seven-furlong Grand Prix de Paris, run over the Longchamp course in the Bois de Boulogne. Lining up with Nearco at the start were English Derby winner, Bois Roussel; French Derby winner, Cillas; French Oaks and One Thousand Guineas winner, Feerie; Prix Lupin winner, Castel Fusano; and the good stayer Canot.

Nearco took the lead early in the straight and galloped away from the rest of the field with his accustomed ease. Coming into the final furlong it appeared Nearco was bounding to victory when a great roar erupted from the packed stands. With 200 yards to go, Canot was taking a run at the Italian champion. Unaccustomed to being challenged, Nearco dug in and battled back. Suddenly, Bois Roussel made a tremendous surge; but Nearco had speed and determination to spare, and flashed across the finish 1-1/2 lengths ahead of the English Derby winner. Nearco's triumph established him as Champion of Europe.

"I stood with Tesio on the stands at Longchamp for the Grand Prix 1938." recalled Mario Incisa della Rochetta. "He stood motionless and silent watching Nearco's every stride as though spurring him on with his eyes. As Nearco sailed effortlessly past the winning post, Tesio let go and, giving me a great thump on the back, he let out a cry of triumph. It was not an 'Oh!' of satisfaction but the full-throated and terrible 'Aaah!' of Attila the Hun.... Tesio's great dream had come true, and thank God, he had lived to see it."

That Nearco features prominently in the world's most influential Thoroughbred bloodlines may have been due to another act of fate. When Tesio journeyed to France with Nearco for the 1938 Grand

Prix de Paris, the clouds of war were hovering over Europe. Rather than bring Nearco back home to Italy, Tesio chose to sell his horse to British bookmaker Martin Benson, for £60,000, the highest price ever paid for a Thoroughbred. Nearco was instantly spirited out of France to the safety of Benson's Beech House Stud at Newmarket, where he would stand and be bred with the finest bloodlines of the time.

Halo, sire of Japan's leading stallion, Sunday Silence, is a great-great-grandson of Nearco; as is Mill Reef, sire of 1978 English Derby winner, Shirley Heights, sire of 1985 English Derby winner, Slip Anchor. Shirley Heights is also the sire of High Hawk, dam of In The Wings, sire of the beautiful champion Singspiel.

Blushing Groom, sire of 1989 English Derby winner, Nashwan, and of 1985 Prix de l'Arc de Triomphe winner, Rainbow Quest, is a great-grandson of Nearco.

Nearco's son, Nasrullah, is the forebear of many great U.S. champions, including Bold Ruler, leading U.S. stallion for seven consecutive years. Bold Ruler was sire of What a Pleasure, Chieftain, Boldnesian, Bold Lad and the peerless Secretariat.

Vaguely Noble, 1968 Prix de l'Arc de Triomphe winner, was the son of Nearco daughter, Noble Lassie. Vaguely Noble was sire to Dahlia, one of the finest racehorses in history. Sir Ivor, 1968 English Derby winner and sire of 1976 Prix de l'Arc de Triomphe winner, Ivanjica, is a great-great grandson of Nearco. Roberto, 1972 English Derby winner, and leading sire has Nearco in the fifth generation on both his dam and sire sides.

And then there is Nearco's great-grandson, Riverman, twice leading sire in France and one of the few stallions to have sired one hundred or more stakes winners. Nearco is also in the pedigree of the important sires Alydar, Mr. Prospector, Seattle Slew, and Habitat. On and on the list goes.

Yet, of all of his male descendants, the son that most resembles Nearco, is Nearctic. He is also the most dominant sire.

PART THREE

END OF ONE ERA —
BEGINNING OF THE NEW

During the first week of March 1953 Nearco and Lady Angela met in the Beech House Stud breeding arena for their fourth encounter. Following the Newmarket sale the previous November, Lady Angela was taken back to Beech House Stud and Martin Benson left for Florida (where his spending money was couriered to him). The following February Lady Angela gave birth to a colt, a son of Nearco.

In late July Lady Angela left her Newmarket home for the last time. She and her tiny foal were walked into a horse van and driven to the docks, where they boarded a freighter bound for Montreal, Canada. Lady Angela was almost five months pregnant.

The day before the ship was scheduled to arrive, Gil Darlington, general manager of E.P. Taylor's new National Stud farm, dispatched stallion manager Harry Green to Montreal to collect three horses arriving from England. One was a gift to Taylor from Lord Derby, the other two were Lady Angela and her foal.

Harry Green was a most remarkable and intuitive horseman, but it was likely his humility that enabled him to work with these great animals. He handled some of the most volatile and demanding stallions—Northern Dancer, Nearctic and the french stallion Menetrier, so violent that when he was led in and out of his paddock someone stood nearby with a loaded rifle, lest the horse decide to savage his handler, Harry Green. The rest of the staff were terrified of the horse. Harry Green may have been part horse: he was always trying to understand them, to see the world from their perspective.

I lived and worked at Windfields Farm estate in Toronto for twelve years riding and training—or being trained by—Taylor's riding horses. Some of my fondest memories are of the hours spent in the tackroom cleaning the bridles and saddles and listening to Harry Green's stories. He was, in so many ways, the history of Windfields Farm.

One of my favourites exemplifies the highly intuitive and instinctual nature of this wonderful man:

Very early each year at Windfields Farm, they bred five or six "nurse mares," usually cold-blooded horses—half-breds, draft horses or quarter horses. For many years they used Fell ponies, the sturdy coal-black miniature draft horses that Taylor often rode. The nurse mares foaled well before the Thoroughbred mares, so if one of the Thoroughbred mares fell ill and was unable to nurse her foal, one of these nurse mares would take over. The nurse mare's foal joined a small band of orphan foals cared for by the Windfields staff. Nurse mares not been required to look after a Thoroughbred foal also remained in this herd, with their own foals.

Harry Green and his wife, Florence lived in a house on the National Stud property. One year Harry became enchanted with one of the tiny orphan foals, and before long he had the foal living in the garage next to his house. On summer evenings, Harry and Florence went for long walks along the lanes between the paddocks, down into the valley and along the riding trails that wound through the forest. They were always accompanied by a menagerie of animals: dogs, cats, the occasional duck, and now, Harry's orphan foal.

Initially Harry fed his foal the same baby formula they fed the other orphan foals, but before long Harry decided that it was time for his foal to eat grass. So off they went, Harry and the foal, into a nearby paddock.

Harry thought his foal would instinctively start eating grass; but no. The foal merely followed him around the paddock, nuzzling at his pockets for a treat. Harry grabbed a handful of what he thought looked like tasty grass and offered it to his foal. He put the grass in his outstretched hand and held it right up to the foal's lips. Still the foal showed no interest.

That evening, when Harry and Florence took their menagerie of animals for their daily stroll around the farm, the answer finally came to him, with thanks to Florence. The problem, she suggested, was that the foal perceived Harry to be its mother.

The following day, after he had completed his chores in the stallion barn, Harry got the foal and brought it out on to the front lawn. Foals, of course, mimic the behaviour of their mothers. Technically, it is called *patterning*.

Since Harry was the foal's chief care-giver, Harry reasoned that it might well mimic him. So Harry got down on his hands and knees and started to graze or, at least, pretend to graze. Eventually the curious foal began to copy him. Problem solved.

Whenever I think about Harry, I picture him in his old tweed cap, and how, when he was flummoxed by the behaviour of a horse he would take off his cap and stroke his shiny bald skull. A skull, incidentally, that bore a scar in the shape of a horse's hoof.

Harry was the stallion manager of the National Stud Farm when Northern Dancer was retired to stud in the fall of 1964. You could almost set your watch by the precise schedule Harry kept for his stallions. They were served breakfast at 6:00 a.m. At 6:30 a.m. Harry began leading his charges out to their paddocks.

It did not take the volatile and sexually-charged young Northern Dancer long to realize what it meant when Harry arrived at his paddock to bring him back into the barn during the breeding season. It meant a trip to the breeding arena. And as Northern Dancer seemed more than willing to breed every mare on the farm, he greeted Harry's appearance with extreme enthusiasm.

Once Harry got the dancing, prancing, hollering stallion back in his stall, he would slip a bridle over Northern Dancer's head and groom him in preparation for his date in the breeding arena.

But one day, the routine was altered. Harry did not plan to accompany Northern Dancer to the breeding arena. It seems that Taylor had unexpectedly arrived at the farm with a number of guests and a magazine photographer who wanted to see Northern Dancer.

Taylor and his guests were gathered on the lawn to the east of the stallion barn; Harry was to bring Northern Dancer to them. But Northern Dancer had a different idea.

As they left the barn Harry turned left toward the guests. Northern Dancer, however, was prepared to charge straight ahead down the path to the breeding arena.

Harry gave a sharp tug on the lead shank, but Northern Dancer was not about to accept discipline from anyone, not even Harry Green, if it meant being led away from the breeding arena.

This was Northern Dancer's first season at stud and even Harry had underestimated how wild this virile young horse could become. By the time Harry realized his mistake, Northern Dancer was confused, frustrated and very angry. Still, Harry thought that if he led Northern Dancer back into the barn and out the doors at the north end—in the opposite direction from the breeding arena—all would be okay.

Harry turned back toward the barn, frustrated not by Northern Dancer's behaviour, but because "The Boss," as Harry called Taylor, was being kept waiting. Northern Dancer, however, had only one thing on his mind.

Harry did not remember what happened next. But Northern Dancer's right front hoof landed squarely on Harry's head, which was protected only by his old tweed cap. Harry got Northern Dancer back into the barn. They marched through to the north doors and on to the lawn where *The Boss* and his friends were standing.

Harry paraded Northern Dancer for the group. Taylor then asked Harry if he could have Northern Dancer stand still so that the magazine photographer could take photographs of him.

"But he wouldn't stand still," Harry recounted, "He was like a spoiled kid. Luro [the trainer] spoiled him. Gave him pounds of those little sugar lumps to bribe him. Northern Dancer did get to be respectful, but it took a bit of doing."

It wasn't until Harry returned Northern Dancer to his stall that he took off his old tweed cap. Blood, which had been contained by the cap, poured down the side of his skull. Harry was rushed to the hospital.

"It took nine stitches to put things back in place. For the next couple of weeks, no matter where he was, Mr. Taylor phoned me every morning. I think he felt pretty bad about what happened."

I never heard Harry boast, and I know that he would blush with embarrassment at the suggestion that he played a pivotal role in the history of the Thoroughbred. Still, only a person with Harry Green's remarkable horse sense could have handled a traumatized Lady Angela, mother of Nearctic, matriarch of this Thoroughbred dynasty.

The horse that Lord Derby had given Taylor was the first off the ship. Harry met the horse, walked it across the dock and secured it in his horse van. He then returned to the pier and sat down on an old wooden crate to wait for his other two passengers.

The longer he waited, the more concerned he became. Lord Derby's horse had been brought to him fairly quickly. Something had to be wrong.

After some time, he noticed a crew member rushing down the gangplank and along the pier toward him. The anxious crew member explained that they were having some difficulty with one of the horses and asked if Harry would come aboard and speak with the first mate.

Harry was brought to the first mate, at the rim of the hatch overlooking the ship's vast hold.

"Even from where I was standing," recalled Harry, "three stories up, I could see that the mare was in a lather. She was frantic, slipping and sliding all over the slippery steel floor."

The ship's officer believed that the mare was crazed and obviously dangerous. He asked Harry if he could help out. The first thing Harry did was shout down to the crew to stop everything and put the mare back in her makeshift stall.

When he arrived in the ship's hold, Lady Angela was quivering in fear and rage. Her dark chestnut hide was white with lather. Sweat was streaming off her body. The crew explained that they had been trying to get her into the shipping crate that would convey her up and out of the ship, but she became frenzied and dangerous.

The more they tried, the more violent she became—and the more frightened they became.

Harry knew absolutely nothing about unloading ships. In fact, he had never before been aboard a ship until that afternoon. He did, however, know as much as anyone on the planet about transporting horses. Harry had been driving a horse van since he was old enough to obtain a driver's licence. As a young man he worked for Toronto veterinarian, Doctor Black, whose veterinary hospital was located on Queen Street near the old Woodbine racetrack.

Harry went right into Lady Angela's stall, talking to her and stroking her. He knew exactly what the problem was. Lady Angela, like all mares, would not go anywhere without her foal.

When Lady Angela was calmed down and breathing normally, Harry explained his plan to the ship's officer: First he would take the foal off the ship and then return for Lady Angela.

The ship's officer, anxious to have this wild animal off his ship, was ready to agree to almost anything, but he did have a problem with Harry staying with the foal during disembarking.

"I was worried that the netting the crew were putting over the crate might frighten the little fellow," recalled Harry, "so I asked the first mate for permission to ride up in the crate with the foal. He finally agreed, as long as I realized they couldn't be responsible if something happened to me."

The little foal was more concerned about being separated from its mother than it was about the ride. It nickered and screamed. But Harry manoeuvered the foal into the crate, the netting was thrown over it, and the perimeter chains fastened to a giant crane up on the main deck.

The crate was hoisted up and out of the cargo area, then swung over the deck and lowered on to the dock.

Harry was none too happy with the ride: "I don't know who was more scared, me or the little foal. Probably me..."

Still, Harry focused on keeping the foal calm. Once he had him secured in the horse van, he ran back to the ship to retrieve Lady Angela. Anxious to get to her foal, Lady Angela walked willingly into the crate, with Harry patting and reassuring her, until they, too, were landed safely on the dock.

Epic's victory in the 1950 King's Plate marked the fourth time in five years that a horse trained over the winter in the southern United States had won the prestigious race. The directors of the Ontario Jockey Club were displeased by this turn of events, and not long after Epic's triumph, they declared that training for the Plate outside Canada would no longer be allowed.

Bert Alexandra went ballistic and was pleased to have his thoughts quoted in an article by Joe Perlove in the *Toronto Star*. Perlove began:

"Meeting in solemn conclave recently, directors of the Ontario Jockey Club took a firm grip on their monocles, adjusted their grey toppers firmly and edicted that for 1951 and henceforth no entrant for the King's Plate would be permitted to train anywhere but within the boundaries of the Dominion.

"No more will E.P. Taylor be able to send a Plate nominee to California, as he did with Epic, to properly warm up to the long, long, grind necessary for a three-year-old to be ready to run nine furlongs early in May...

"None of that, said they. Henceforth ye shall drag that horse out of the cold, cold barn into zero weather and get him going over ice and snow. In effect they said, "We'll improve the breed if we have to break down every horse which tries the "Plate."

Perlove then quoted prominent Thoroughbred owner, Carr Hatch, who also thought the new ruling was ridiculous:

"I am dead against it... To my mind the rule was pushed through by a couple of chiselers on the board, who run horses but don't want to spend too much money at it."

Then Perlove quoted Bert Alexandra:

"They should be horsewhipped. It is the most disgraceful thing I've ever heard. They want to make sure we break the horse down. I never liked the Plate at any time. Not the way it's run. You did have a little better chance to bring a horse to the race properly with training down south.

"They're worrying about the little man?" Bert rolled on. "From what I recall the little man is lucky to get stalls at the Woodbine... The racetrack wasn't made for the little men. Most little men make money at the track. It's the big man who spends the money, and makes the racetrack. They'd look good without Mr. Taylor, R.S. McLaughlin, and fellows like that."

Perlove concluded: "Brother Bert has retired for the winter and admits it might be a long winter. Meaning he may hang up his bandages for good."

The following spring Bert's wife received a letter from the secretary of Ontario Jockey Club, denying Bert's request for passes, citing his comments in the newspaper column as the reason:

"If your husband feels inclined to deny these statements, or if he admits having made them and is prepared to write an apology to the Board of Directors of the Ontario Jockey Club, the matter will come up for further consideration at an early meeting of my Board."

Bert, of course, refused to apologize, and retired—this time, permanently.

Fortune, however, had smiled on Taylor, for the past fourteen years, ever since Bert agreed to postpone his retirement to help him build a racing stable. Training Thoroughbreds was not then a particularly lucrative profession, and these were particularly tough times for the Canadian Thoroughbred sport. So it's highly unlikely that the Cosgrave Stable experiment would have grown into Windfields Farm and eventual domination of Thoroughbred breeding had Bert not been in command.

He assembled a racing stable, almost overnight, and took E.P.

Taylor's fledgling Cosgrave stable straight to the top—winning race after race, often by Alexandra's sheer cunning. Each time one of his horses won, Taylor became more enchanted, more committed.

Bert, of course, trained Mona Bell, star of the Cosgrave runners. Her victories in Canada and the United States were the main impetus of the success and supremacy of the fledgling racing stable. At three, Mona Bell won seven races and was second six times, including the 1938 King's Plate: the filly led the field for the first mile, only to be overtaken by Bunty Lawless in the final quarter.

By mid-August 1939, her four-year-old season, Mona Bell was out of the money only twice in eleven starts. Her victories included the Orpen Memorial Handicap in which she had beaten Bunty Lawless. At this point it was announced that, upon retirement, these two horses would be bred to each other, and fans of horse racing reacted as though the announcement was the engagement of two local celebrities.

Mona Bell and the excitement she generated, raised Taylor's sights, inspiring him to breed his own horses. Indeed, many great Thoroughbreds trace their roots back to the decision to breed Mona Bell and Bunty Lawless.

It was Bert Alexandra who bought Nandi on his first trip to Maryland for Taylor back in 1936, and who trained Windfields and Epic, the Taylors' first Queen's Plate winner.

At the time, Bert certainly had more money than Taylor, at least more available cash. As most of Taylor's money was tied up in getting his business up and running, there were periods when Bert Alexandra was bankrolling almost the entire racing stable operation. Taylor referred to Bert Alexandra as his "banker." It is doubtful whether he could have continued his racing stable dream without the financial assistance of Bert Alexandra.

However, Bert Alexandra's greatest contribution may well have been in giving Edward and Winifred Taylor so many thrilling victories and good times. That this was all achieved at a profit, no doubt appealed to Taylor's entrepreneurial spirit.

One evening Mrs. Taylor told me stories from the time of Bert Alexandra. Her blue eyes sparkled with delight as she recalled some of Bert's antics.

"Oh, we had such fun in those days," she reminisced. "Oh, I know Eddie had to change things—conditions for the horses were very poor, and that part is so much better now. But, I do miss those early days. I miss the laughter. And all the fun and excitement."

The last time I saw Bert Alexandra and his wife Bea was in the summer of 1977. They had called ahead to say that they would be in town on their annual excursion to Canada to celebrate Bert's birthday, so I arranged lunch at Woodbine racetrack with Mr. and Mrs. Taylor. I thought it would be great fun to get them together after all these years to reminisce about the "good old days."

My plan worked, but not entirely. Bert Alexandra was more than happy to reminisce, as were Mrs. Taylor and Mrs. Alexandra. At one point, Bert was telling quite a humorous story that involved a betting coup, Taylor, and a bit of good-natured mischief. Taylor, sitting across the table, was clearly not amused. Finally he said, "You can't believe anything told to you by a man who hasn't worked for over twenty-five years." Shortly thereafter, Taylor excused himself from the table on the grounds that he "had some business to attend to."

That day confirmed the divergent natures of these two men. Bert Alexandra, who retired in his late forties, was totally content with his life of leisure. E.P. Taylor restlessly worked and dreamed and schemed, daily, until his early eighties when he was felled by a debilitating stroke.

Still, in the early days these two personalities had meshed; for fourteen years they experienced great success and great fun. But by 1950 they were at a fork in the road. Bert had so successfully initiated Taylor into Thoroughbred sport that Taylor would spend the rest of his life committed to it. Bert Alexandra had been brilliant in his role, but now it was time for him to depart. So he stomped off, muttering about what a bunch of imbeciles sat on the board of the Ontario Jockey Club.

"Of all Nearco's sons with racing class, Nearctic bears
the closest resemblance to his sire."

JOHN AISCAN, THE BRITISH RACEHORSE

Lady Angela gave birth to her fourth foal sired by Nearco at
10:30 a.m. 11 February 1954, at Windfields Farm. At the time,
concern over virus abortion led all the Taylor mares to be vanned
from the National Stud farm in Oshawa to Toronto to foal.

Officially, Bill Reeves was the Windfields Farm broodmare
manager. His job was to assist the mares while they were giving
birth to their foals. As most mares foal between 11:00 p.m. and 2:30
a.m., for five months of the year, starting late January, Reeves worked
the night shift. He still found time for his first love—riding. He
exercised some of the stallions, and in the fall, he helped out with
the yearlings.

The morning Nearctic was born, Reeves was in the stallion barn
putting the tack on Bull Page, grandsire of Nijinsky.

"I used to ride Bull Page," explained Reeves. "We found that
exercise was good for the stallions. It also made them a lot easier to
work with.

"So I was just about to go out with Bull Page when someone
hollered that Lady Angela was getting ready to foal. She was out in
a paddock close to her barn and walking around and around. They
brought her in to her stall, and not long after I arrived, she lay down.

"I don't remember any complications. I think it must have been
an easy foaling. Lady Angela was a really nice mare. She was

easygoing, a pleasure to work around. She had no problems, no bad habits. You'd remember her just for her personality. And she was a good mother."

Lady Angela's foal was a sturdy colt with good bone and solid hindquarters. His coat was dark, almost black; he had a small vee-shaped white marking in the centre of his round forehead and a snip of white at the top of his muzzle. Short white socks capped his hind legs from the top of his tiny hooves over the fetlocks.

"He was a big black colt." recalled Reeves, "And he had the *look*. He would stare at you—as if to say 'I am the king.'"

According to former Windfields Farm yearling manager, Andre Blaettler, this colt was "a real tough son of a gun: I remember this time when we had to give him some shots. He was four months old. There was this very big guy who was supposed to hold him. But the guy couldn't hold him. The colt was just that tough!"

Bill Reeves also remembered the incident.

"The big guy was the vet, Dr. Caverly. We were trying to worm Nearctic with a tube. He was just a weanling. He wasn't that big yet, but he fought back. We never did tube him, the little sucker..."

"The other thing I remember about Nearctic as a foal," added Blaettler, "is that he didn't follow the mare [Lady Angela] around. Instead he would be standing at the gate, on his own."

Nearctic's atypical independence should not be surprising. Both his sire, Nearco, and his grandsire, Hyperion, were extremely independent; yet, such independence is highly unusual. Horses are flight animals, dependent upon the herd for their very survival. The dynamics of the group that factor significantly in the make-up of each individual horse often also play out in a horse race. The safest place to be in a herd escaping from a predator is in the middle of the pack. Stragglers are most vulnerable to being picked off. Those who get too far ahead of the herd are also at risk.

Apply this paradigm to a horse race: In most instances the winner cruises along in the middle of the field until its jockey urges the horse to leave the pack in the final stretch. Thus the final furlong, and therefore, the winner's circle belong to the horse with the greatest stamina and the will.

Foals are particularly affected by herd dynamics. They are born blind and it generally takes two days for their eyesight to develop fully. In the wild, the entire herd will visit the newborn foal, one by one. Each will blow into the foal's nostrils. As horses have extraordinary olfactory capacities, during its first vulnerable days the foal will use its sense of smell to identify its herd.

Foals are born with legs two-thirds their adult length, so that they can cover the same amount of ground at the gallop as their mothers. Within no time at all on their first outing, the foals are doing precisely that, running alongside their mothers, matching them, stride for stride.

In the beginning foals seldom stray far from their mothers' sides. It is as if there is an invisible boundary—the "mom zone," around the mare—within which the foal feels safe. With most foals, for the first few weeks, mom zone extends only a few feet away from the mare. Foals may wander past this circumference, but will suddenly come running back to safety. And the mare is, as a rule, vigilant and ready to defend her youngster.

With most mares, her body language says it all. Her ears are pinned flat back, her neck outstretched, her teeth bared. The message is clear—stay away from my baby! The occasional mare, however, can be downright nasty, even dangerous if they are threatened. These mares, or their dams, have suffered some trauma, invariably at the hands of humans, that has made them entirely distrusting.

As the weeks go by and the foal grows in stature and confidence, the "mom zone" expands. Ever curious and energetic, the foal begins cavorting with the other foals. When their energy is spent, they return to their mothers, collapse onto the grass and fall into a deep sleep, as their ever-vigilant mothers stand guard. Once recharged, the foals scramble back up onto their long legs to resume their games.

When Andre Blaettler told me about Nearctic's apparent independence from his mother, I recalled something I had read in the *British Racehorse* magazine. The article was published in May 1975 and was written by John Aiscan.

It was the opinion of Aiscan that: "of all Nearco's sons, he [Nearctic] bears the closest resemblance to his sire...Nearctic had the same head and same expression as Nearco. He was a bit bigger and stronger...

"Nearctic is the best horse to come from the mating of Nearco with a Hyperion mare... Great hopes were predicted of successful matings between Nearco and Hyperion mares, but the cross of those two great sires did not create any greatness. Nearctic was the best result.

"Why did this mating not live up to expectations? The main reason: according to Tesio, Nearco was a self-willed type of horse, and Hyperion also had an independent nature. Probably this type of mating resulted in too much mental refinement. Mental over-refinement results in horses with too much nervous energy...

"Horses by sons or grandsons of Nearco out of mares by sons or grandsons of Hyperion have less character and temperament problems. Thus we can see the improvement in mental characteristics of this particular mating from generation to generation."

Given both Hyperion's and Nearco's extreme independence, this theory makes sense.

"All Thoroughbreds, however, be they good, mediocre or poor racehorses, show a definite family resemblance," wrote Tesio in *Breeding the Race-Horse*. "They all have two elements in common— a high degree of nervous energy and a certain 'quality' derived from selection. The fact that these two characteristics appear in all Thoroughbreds indicates that they are not inherited according to the law of Mendel, but are passed directly from parents to offspring."

In order to study the complexities of heredity in direct line, he embarked upon an extensive examination of the two horse races he considered the most significant in the development of the Thoroughbred—the English Derby and the English Oaks. Both run at Epsom Downs, the English Derby was contested for the first time in the year 1780 and the English Oaks, in 1779.

Tesio conducted this study in 1939, and discovered that, up to that time, 80 per cent of the colts that had won the English Derby "were by stallions who, although they were animals of quality, had not themselves won the Derby. I also found that certain famous Derby winning stallions had as many as four Derby winning sons.

"But it has never happened that sire, son, grandson and great-grandson—in other words, four consecutive generations in direct male line—have won the Derby."

Tesio found similar results in the English Oaks: "It has never happened that dam, daughter, granddaughter and great-granddaughter consecutively have won The Oaks. The sequence has reached the third generation at the most—never the fourth."

In conclusion Tesio states that over the English Oaks and English Derby period frame he examined "approximately a million horses were eligible to attempt the battle for the Derby Crown at Epsom. 161 were winners and these formed the dominant class of selected producers. But not one of them has ever been able to establish the supremacy of his family for more than three generations in direct line. It would seem that the number 3 has a special significance, but even if a fourth generation should crop up it would not alter the law itself.

"If it were not for this law, which sets a limit to the evolution of individual lines of inheritance by restricting it to limited cycles, the established order of things would soon be upset. By means of hybridism, selection and evolution, man could develop peas as big as pumpkins and pumpkins as small as peas."

The final paragraph in Tesio's analysis echos the essence of

Nearctic:

"Breeders have always concentrated on improving the speed of the Thoroughbred, which is not a Mendelian character but is derived from a combination of many Mendelian characters under the influence of nervous energy. These characters, by selection through the severe test of the races, have all been stamped with the mark of quality. But through successive generations the degree of nervous energy and of selected quality can only reach a certain limit. When this limit is reached, the 'bubble' must burst."

With Nearctic, Thoroughbred breeding reached, or perhaps even went a bit beyond, that certain limit. I suspect that Nearctic sits perched, no doubt precariously, at the pinnacle, in terms of the degree of nervous energy and selected quality. His genetic makeup was so perfect, so dynamic, so explosive, that he was like a genetic time-bomb.

This inherent volatility might also help to explain why the others that were offshoots of this genetic formula did not make it as racehorses.

Monday evening, 22 August 1955 Nearctic, then known simply as the Nearco/Lady Angela colt, joined the Thoroughbred yearlings at Taylor's annual sale. It was the first cool evening after a lengthy bout of hot and humid weather.

The Nearco/Lady Angela colt, tall and rangy, carried a $35,000 price tag, the amount Taylor had paid for the colt's mother, Lady Angela. In Newmarket, $35,000 had been considered a lot of money for a horse; in Canada, it was unheard of. It is probably safe to assume that Taylor did not want to sell this colt.

M.J. Boylen, a Canadian mining promoter, showed some interest in the colt, but was talked out of buying him by his trainer, Art Warner. (Seven years later, Warner talked Boylen's sons, Jim and Phil, out of buying Northern Dancer as a yearling.)

The previous spring Taylor found himself with almost forty yearlings, far too many for one racing stable to contend with. He therefore devised a plan that was a departure from the conventional method of selling horses, i.e., consigning them to an auction of yearlings.

Taylor's plan was original, creative, and ultimately, a factor in the unprecedented success of his Windfields Farm. He decided to offer the entire crop of yearlings at predetermined prices. A catalogue was prepared like that of a public yearling auction, and the event was staged at his Windfields Farm. As he intended to continue racing his horses, he deemed that the sale would conclude when half the fillies and half the colts had been sold. The remaining horses would run under Windfields' turquoise and gold racing colours. He then drew up a list of friends, associates in racing, and others whom he thought would be interested, and invited them to his sale.

Selecting his buyers was a brilliant strategy: It assured him of getting his horses into the best stables and therefore every opportunity to prove themselves.

In the inaugural year, Taylor offered thirty-five yearlings. Five colts and four fillies were sold. Bill Beasley, proprietor of an amusement company, bought two of the youngsters. One, a bay colt sired by Windfields out of the mare Bolesteo cost Beasley $7,500. Beasley named the colt Canadian Champ.

Now, at the time of Taylor's second annual sale, Canadian Champ was a two-year-old and was proving to be a stellar racehorse. He would go on to win Canada's top juvenile races, and the following year, the Queen's Plate. In the meantime, Canadian Champ provided an incentive to attend Taylor's sale. Taylor's horses were expensive, more than most Canadians were prepared to pay; but Taylor was breeding some very good horses.

Still, the $35,000 asking price for Nearctic was considered a fortune: The average paid at the 1955 Canadian Thoroughbred Horse Society Sale was $2,392.

Nearctic's full-brother, Empire Day, the foal that accompanied Lady Angela from England, was now a two-year-old. He had, however, started only once prior to the sale. In July he sprinted five furlongs and won the maiden event by one-and-a-half furlongs. Empire Day did not run again until September, when he finished seventh.

Perhaps had Empire Day been a top two-year-old, there might have been a bit of incentive to pay that $35,000 for his beautifully-bred brother; but it is unlikely. While many Canadian Thoroughbred owners were quite wealthy, when it came to buying horses, they had shallow pockets.

That the Nearco/Lady Angela colt looked very much like his famous sire probably didn't impress buyers either—few among them knew what Nearco looked like. Instead, the buyers purchased the less expensive yearlings—horses by stallions with whom they were familiar.

And so it was that the Lady Angela/Nearco colt stayed at Windfields Farm. Winifred Taylor named him Nearctic. It was obviously a play on the name of his sire, Nearco, and the perception of many people south of the 49th parallel, that Canada was situated on the tundra.

In 1958, several years after Winifred Taylor named her horse, "nearctic" was entered in the dictionary, not as a proper noun, but as an adjective. Its refers to the biogeographic region that begins north of tropical Mexico and encompasses the rest of North America and Greenland. The influence of Nearctic the horse, however, would spread over a far larger land mass.

The decade of the fifties heralded a whole new chapter in the history of Canadian Thoroughbred sport. With E.P. Taylor at the helm, everything would change, so much so, that, by the end of the decade, Canadian Thoroughbred racing had been transformed. Taylor was surely a man with a mission. One his first tasks, however, was to replace Bert Alexandra. So, he sought the advice of Gil Darlington, who recommended Gordon (Pete) McCann.

"If I had my choice of all the trainers on the Canadian circuit," Darlington replied, "this fellow is the one that would have my horses, especially if the majority of them were two- and three-year-olds. He's good with any kind of horse, but stands out in this department."

If McCann had any faults, Darlington wrote, "It may sound funny, but actually he has been too loyal and honest to suit the majority of owners. He won't sell ten-dollar bills for a quarter. He's the most bashful horseman I have come across."

Indeed, Pete McCann was the antithesis of Bert Alexandra. Where Alexandra was volatile, mischievous and outspoken, McCann was withdrawn, modest, and taciturn.

A former jockey, he began his riding career at the small country fairs that are a long-time tradition in rural Ontario. Celebrating the completion of the fall harvest, usually lasting several days, the fairs include midway rides for the children, pie baking competitions, games of chance, judging of cattle, sheep and poultry; prizes for the largest pumpkin, equestrian events, and horse races.

In those early days, Pete McCann walked his horse from his family home on the eastern fringes of Toronto to the village of Markham where there was a permanent track on the Markham

Fairgrounds. The return trip was about thirty miles. Later on, he rode on the bigger Ontario racetracks, followed by several seasons in Cuba. One afternoon at Havana's Orientale Park Pete rode four winners. He was Cuba's leading rider in 1926.

Pete McCann would not say he was a top rider. Indeed, Pete wouldn't say two words when one would do. Still, his reputation was legend.

"Pete sure could horse back," says Bill Reeves, a former jockey and assistant trainer to McCann for eleven years. "And Pete sure was game. Back in those days you would be paid fifty cents a gallop. There was this horse, Tullamore, owned by Bill MacDonald. No one could ride him except Pete. The horse was a real rough one, crazy. MacDonald paid Pete ten dollars to gallop him."

Pete rode a horse called Listerine in the 1927 King's Plate, but finished out of the money. In 1930 he was fourth on Vestip. When keeping his weight down became too difficult Pete turned to riding steeplechase horses.

In the fall of 1939, Willie Morrissey, the volatile Toronto tavern owner, fired his trainer and hired Pete. Included in Morrissey's string were Bunty Lawless and his full-brother, Willie the Kid.

Not entirely sound, Willie the Kid did not race as a two-year-old. "He had everything against him," said Pete, in one of his rare statements. Nonetheless, every morning throughout the winter of 1939, Pete galloped Willie the Kid over the Old Dufferin Park track. Pete's intent was to build up Willie the Kid's muscles and cardiovascular capacity to compensate for his physical weaknesses.

He galloped Willie the Kid at least five or six miles a day, no matter the weather. Rain, sleet, snow storms, ice storms, Willie the Kid never missed a gallop. So when Willie the Kid lined up with the ten other horses for the 1940 King's Plate, the colt was as fit as a prize fighter. Still this was his racing debut. Ring Wise, a colt owned by Harry Giddings was the favourite.

For the first time, the new Clay Puett starting gate would be used for the King's Plate. As the starter rang the starting bell, Ring Wise backed out of his stall and left facing the wrong direction as the rest of the horses went galloping down the track. Willie the Kid galloped easily with the leaders and in the final turn took control. Young Pete McCann had his first Plate winner. The first of many.

Willie the Kid's victory was due to luck and conditioning. Perhaps it was at this time that Pete fully understood the benefits of conditioning, because his horses were fit—possibly the fittest horses on the North American circuit. It was a source of pride. In fact, the closest I ever heard Pete McCann come to bragging was when he confided "Conn Smythe said I had the fittest horses he'd ever seen."

Owner of Thoroughbreds and the Maple Leaf hockey team, Smythe was not the only person to recognize Pete's ability to condition his horses. Ron Turcotte, the great Hall of Fame jockey who rode Secretariat, Riva Ridge, and started Northern Dancer, calls McCann "the greatest horse trainer who ever lived."

It was McCann who gave young Turcotte his start with horses in May 1960, and later encouraged Turcotte to become a jockey. Turcotte recalled Pete McCann as a complete horseman who offered him valuable advice and a role model when it came to excellence with horses.

"I started walking hots for Mr. McCann. After a week he said "Ronnie, it's a waste of your talent to be holding a shank," so he gave me two horses and two ponies to groom. A week later, he gave the two ponies to the hot walkers, and he gave me two more horses, so I had four.

"Mr. McCann did all the feeding, and he knew the importance of feeding different quantities to different horses. He gave each horse plenty of time to digest the food. Mr. McCann also was there for the afternoon feeding and at nine at night for watering and to look in. He wasn't afraid to work on a horse's legs either."

In August Pete sent Turcotte to Windfields to learn to ride young horses. "Mr. McCann spent the winter at the farm and he got on the tough horses and was as good as I've ever seen. That's how I learned.

"He told me, 'There's no way a 125-pound man can out-muscle a 1,000- or 1,200-pound Thoroughbred, so you have to learn how to give and take when galloping them.'"

Pete McCann was an excellent and intuitive rider. He generally worked the racehorses himself in the morning. Not all of them— just the good ones, the tough ones, the difficult ones. He understood them at a level beyond that of all other horse trainers.

In fact, beyond all other riders.

I wrote a profile of Pete McCann in the *Toronto Star* in May 1985.

The morning I spent with Pete before writing it is my most cherished memory of this remarkable man. The story was titled, "Octogenarian Pete McCann still top trainer," and I think in many ways it surely summed up the essence of this remarkable horse trainer:

It's 5:15 a.m. The backstretch at Woodbine racetrack is cloaked in dark and eerie silence. I am looking for trainer Pete McCann. I have been told that he and his small band of horses have been moved in to the yearling sales stalls on the other side of the backstretch.

As I drive along the deserted roads between the long rows of stables, I wonder what the man who has trained ten Queen's Plate winners, seven Horses of the Year and Canada's only two [to that time] Triple Crown winners, New Providence and Cannebora, has done to get himself relegated to this inferior stabling.

When I finally arrive in the sales barn area, I begin to search for my hero with some trepidation and considerable difficulty as the area is very dimly lit. Then to the west I see a horse and rider. Like a mirage they are illuminated by a single overhead lightbulb and then disappear into the darkness.

Pete McCann always rode the horses he trained. Nearctic, Canadiana and Viceregal were but some of his mounts.

I am stunned to see him riding. He must be at least eighty years old.

"Well, he was 73 for a few years," confides his assistant, Bud Olsen, "and then last year he finally went to 74. But I wouldn't be surprised if there was an eight in the number, and I don't mean 78..."

By the time I find Pete he has just brought back his second horse of the morning and was about to get on the third. Pete has been here since 4:30 a.m.

"I like to get an early start and get out of here before the crowds arrive," Pete explains, "but they (the Ontario Jockey Club) don't open the training track until six (a.m.). I guess those fellows don't want to get up too early."

The third mount, a very green and nervous two-year-old, shies and bucks only seconds after Olsen has tossed Pete up on to the back of the horse. Pete remains glued to the saddle.

"I have never seen a man that could sit a horse like that one," Bud Olsen says.

Riding a Thoroughbred, especially a young Thoroughbred can be like sitting on a powder keg. Two-year-olds can be high-voltage, temperamental and can explode at the slightest disturbance. One minute you are sitting in the saddle and the next the world collapses out from beneath you. You hit the ground hard enough to knock the air out of your lungs. If you are lucky you won't have broken anything and you will have fallen clear of the horse.

To play this part of the horse game—to ride and train

two-year-old Thoroughbreds before dawn at Woodbine, takes exceptional balance, fitness and talent. To play this part of the horse game at the age of eighty-something is unheard of.

I knew that Pete McCann was still training a few horses, but even in my wildest imagination, I couldn't conceive that he would still be riding. Racehorses. Two-year-olds. Good grief! I truly cannot believe what I am seeing.

Pete tells me that he is going to loosen up his third horse over on the sand ring (a small oval track not far from the stables) and then he will ride the horse over to the training track. Pete's timing is such that the training track would just open when we arrive. Pete McCann and the two-year-old would be the first ones on the track.

But, first to the sand ring. The sun is not yet up, but it is getting lighter. I follow along behind Pete McCann and his horse as they head toward the sand ring. No sooner has Pete got the youngster trotting along the sand when the place erupts. It seems that a small flock of very large, and, soon to be, very noisy, Canada Geese had decided that the centre of this sand ring would be a perfect nesting place. Enraged at the intrusion, and prepared to fight to protect their nesting area, the Canada Geese start flapping their huge wings, and hollering wildly. A couple of them are stomping and flapping and hollering in the direction of Pete and the horse.

The poor horse freaks out. Naturally. Horses are flight animals. These massive and angry birds scare me. Like the horse, I too think I should run for my life. But then I think about Pete. His horse is going mental, trying to escape from the geese. Pete is eighty-something years old. I think I'd better stick around in case he needs my help.

I think wrong.

The two-year-old spins. It bucks. It jumps. It dives. It

almost turns itself inside-out trying to escape from the attacking geese. But Pete McCann remains glued to the saddle.

I stand, my mouth agape, in awe.

Pete is talking to the terrified young horse, guiding it. He is gentle, yet firm. Soon he has restored its confidence, or at least its trust in Pete McCann, to protect it from the monstrous geese.

Pete McCann is a small man. He has strong weathered hands, and his eyes are bright and sparkle with delight and mischief. He is wearing an old beige bowl-type helmet.

"It belonged to Jimmy Fitzsimmons," he boasts proudly.

Under the helmet he wears a wool toque to ward off the cold. He is dressed in a light green quilted jacket, grey over-sized work trousers and looks as if he has just ridden straight off the pages of a Dick Francis mystery novel.

From the geese's homestead we head off in the direction of the training track. When we arrive the racing officials are just removing the barrier. Pete McCann and the high-strung bay colt work a mile over the dirt training track.

The horse gallops strongly down the stretch and Pete sits close to the horse's flying mane, his strong and lithe body springing along easily with each bounding stride.

He appears to be a man who is exactly where he is meant to be, racing the wind on the back of a powerful and unpredictable Thoroughbred.

The sun has just come up and the backstretch has suddenly burst into action. Pete's "crowds" have arrived, or have rolled out of their racetrack bunks. There are horses everywhere. Some are being led, some are being ridden. They prance, snort and rear as they head out toward the training track. Several have already dumped their riders and are galloping wildly around the stable area creating havoc.

The grooms are mucking out the stalls. The trainers are supervising the morning workouts. Those few trainers that do ride, rest assured, are not riding two-year-old Thoroughbreds. Nope. Their mounts are lead ponies— aged, cold-blooded, gentle creatures. And these trainers are sitting on comfortable western saddles. Compared to a light-weight exercise saddle, western saddles are like riding in an armchair.

There is not a trainer that I know of, then or now, who could duplicate what Pete McCann was doing. Not even trainers half his age.

So as the backstretch comes to life, Pete McCann has already finished for the day. And so we sit on a pile of straw bales and Pete McCann talks, and talks. And I listen. It seems to me that he talked more that one morning, than he has talked in his entire lifetime.

You see, Pete McCann, as Gil Darlington had aptly described him, is "the most bashful horseman I have come across." And, that was the problem.

Pete McCann was E.P. Taylor's Canadian trainer from 1950 to 1970 and during that time the Windfields turquoise and gold racing silks dominated the winner's circle at Woodbine.

In 1970, Pete McCann was retired and the racehorses were distributed to a number of public trainers. It wasn't long before the Windfields racers were no longer a major threat on either the Canadian or U.S. Thoroughbred circuits.

Pete McCann, retired or not, kept on training, but no one would send him their horses. Which is unfortunate, particularly for the horses, for Pete McCann had certainly proven himself as the finest trainer of Thoroughbreds this country has ever produced.

Pete, of course, would be the last person to tell you.

The training of Thoroughbreds in North America, is in some ways a most curious occupation. Often, people like Pete McCann, the really talented ones, are overlooked by the horse owners, in favour of more glamorous trainers whose greatest talent may be outstanding salesmanship and showmanship. They know their clients, and they know how to keep them happy.

Pete McCann, thought his job was to keep the Windfields horses fit, healthy and winning. But despite his extraordinary ability with Thoroughbreds Pete lost his job.

> "With Pete, Nearctic had the potential to be a great
> horse, without Pete, Nearctic would not have even
> been a decent racehorse. Pete brought out the best
> in him over and over."

BILL REEVES

Not long after the 1955 yearling sale, Pete began working with the
small herd of yearlings that would run for Windfields Farm. Nearctic
was among this group.

Pete had his own particular way of working with and gentling
young horses. He did not believe in longeing or long-lining or
driving or chasing them around a round pen.

"He didn't believe in tiring them out," explained Bill Reeves, Pete's
assistant for many years, "doing things they will never have to do—
things, he figured, they weren't meant to do."

He preferred one-on-one, close contact. He and his assistants
spent several days in the stall with each of the young horses, treating
each one as an individual. However much time they needed to adjust
to this new turn of events in their young lives, they got. Tack was
put on and taken off. The adjustment to carrying weight was made
by someone lying across their backs, sliding off and on again.

E.P. Taylor's assistant, Beth Heriot, had heard about Pete's magical
way with the young horses, so one day she decided to see for herself.

"It was really amazing," she recalled, "but it is hard to explain. I
remember that he was working with a filly that morning. The filly

seemed very nervous, anxious. I don't actually know how he did it, but he calmed her right down. All I could see him doing was patting her and talking to her. But you could actually see her start to relax. It looked as if she trusted him. That was such a long time ago, but it was one of the moments that you never forget."

Pete McCann was an extraordinarily instinctive horseman. Long before the current spate of professional horse listeners and horse whispers, Pete McCann was talking to his horses, and they were talking to him. Or maybe they were singing.

"Pete talked to his horses with his hands. Pete was smart, intelligent, but his greatest gift was his hands," asserted Reeves. "Pete had great hands. Pete also had the greatest knack in the world of picking a yearling. When you came into the barn and saw Pete's tack outside a stall, you had to know that this horse was going to be a good one. He chose to ride the good ones. How did he know? I can't say, but I saw it over and over. Pete just *knew*."

Pete rode Nearctic nearly every day for almost five years, except when the horse was taken from him, but as soon as he was returned, Pete was back aboard Nearctic.

The only other time Pete didn't begin his day riding Nearctic was when Pete broke his ankle. His entire foot was in a cast, the plaster far too bulky to fit into the stirrup iron.

"So I got to ride Nearctic," recalled Reeves, "But not for long. Still I considered it an honour that he let me ride Nearctic. Nearctic was tough, but riding him was beautiful. Like sitting at a stoplight and the guy next to you is in a Ford Pinto, and you are in a Cadillac— just press the button and I am gone! Zoom!"

Reeves's days in Nearctic's saddle were short-lived. Anxious to get back riding *his* horse, Pete took only three days to rig up an alternative stirrup iron. He found a good long stirrup leather, wrapped it around his cast as a substitute for the iron, and then hooked the leather back to the saddle once he was up on Nearctic.

"That will just show you that he trusted Nearctic, or at least trusted that the horse wouldn't do anything to hurt him," added Reeves.

Bill Reeves was born in Toronto's East York, about two-and-a-half miles from Pete McCann's birthplace in Scarborough. At the time, the Toronto area was rife with racetracks. On the weekends, Reeves and his pals would scurry down the back lanes behind Thorncliffe Park, to sneak into the backstretch and get work as hot walkers.

"We all wanted to be jockeys," reminisced Reeves. "It looked like the most glamorous and exciting job in the world. So when I was fourteen I left home and set out for a life on the track."

Reeves rode professionally from 1945 to 1948, but retired when weight became a problem: "I was simply too big, and I don't think I was very good. But it was the greatest thrill — sitting on the back of a horse in the starting gate, hearing the bell, flying down the track. There is nothing like it."

When Reeves hung up his tack he tried his hand at an assortment of jobs, but nothing held any real appeal. After several years Reeves phoned Gil Darlington and told him he wanted to get back working with horses. The timing was perfect. Several months earlier, E.P. Taylor had hired Darlington as general manager of his new National Stud Farm. In the reorganization of Taylor's two farms, they would need someone at Windfields in Toronto to look after the broodmares.

In 1951, Reeves began his lengthy Windfields tenure, responsible for foaling the mares. The foaling season stretched from late January to late May, and when Pete McCann began working with the yearlings in the fall, Reeves joined the yearling crew.

"One of the things I remember about those days is that when you were working with a horse, especially a difficult horse, Pete would never leave you. Lots of trainers would just walk away, leave you on your own," recalled Reeves, "but Pete would always be there."

One morning in the spring of 1959, E. P. Taylor drove out to

Woodbine backstretch to see his horses and decided that Pete needed an assistant.

"Either you find one," said Taylor to Pete, "or I will find one for you."

Pete chose Bill Reeves.

"Mr. Taylor called me into his office and said, 'Pete needs help, back at the farm. He has far too many horses for one man to handle. So you will be his assistant.' And I thought 'Great! What a great opportunity!'"

And indeed it was. Pete was not only a very gifted horse trainer, he was a very unusual horse trainer in that he rode the horses he trained, at least all the good ones. It is possible to gain a good understanding of a horse by working with it on the ground— grooming, feeding and caring for the animal. But riding the horse adds a valuable dimension, one that enriches understanding of that individual, especially if the animal is a racehorse. With a racehorse as combustible and complex as Nearctic, this depth of understanding was critical.

If there was a barometer to measure nervous energy in Thoroughbreds, Nearctic would have been off the scale. Nearctic was always teetering on the edge and therefore not an easy horse.

Yet, the very characteristics that made him so difficult were the very ones that made him the supreme stallion. He was strong, courageous and fearless. Neither pain nor exhaustion stopped him from running his heart out. And Nearctic was a fighter. You could see it in the way he ran. His body language.

Still, Pete didn't believe in fighting his horses. He told me that when he rode Nearctic out in the mornings, he used a double bridle. This is a bridle with two bits—a bridoon bit (jointed in the centre like a regular snaffle bit) and a straight curb bit—and two sets of reins. Fitted to the straight curb bit is a curb-chain that runs beneath the horse's chin. The combination of the two bits, two sets of reins, and curb-chain gives the rider much greater leverage than an ordinary racing snaffle bit, generally used on racehorses. (The double bridle is used on a Grand Prix dressage horse, where control of the animal's energy is essential.)

By using such an extreme bit, Pete could control Nearctic's vast and generally volatile energy on his early morning gallops. When Nearctic raced, however, they went back to using the simple racing snaffle.

PART FOUR

NEARCTIC'S RACING YEARS

Nearctic's racing debut occurred in the third race on a cloudy and cool spring afternoon at the historic racetrack located on the Toronto waterfront. The original track and its adjacent roadhouse were built in 1874, but before long it had attracted an element of shady characters accustomed to cheating. Several years later the roadhouse and grandstand burned to the ground. Joe Duggan, owner of the Woodbine racecourse seized the opportunity to "revive racing in Toronto under respectable auspices and make a success of it." To that end he turned to Sir Casimir Gzowski, aide-de-camp to Queen Victoria. Before long Duggan and Gzowski established the Ontario Jockey Club, and convinced Queen Victoria that the Queen's Plate, the horse race run under royal patronage, should to be confined to one racetrack, and controlled by the Ontario Jockey Club.

In 1947 E. P. Taylor became a director of the Ontario Jockey Club. In the name of the OJC, he had been buying up all the racetracks in the Toronto area. He transferred most of their racing charters—the days, by law, they were allowed to conduct racing—to the Ontario Jockey Club, and sold the properties. He kept only the Fort Erie and Woodbine tracks, and refurbished them. In 1953 Taylor purchased 800 acres at the north end of Toronto and set out to build a "super track" to be named the New Woodbine and scheduled to open in June 1956. But by May the horses had already moved into the backstretch of the new track, so Pete McCann had to walk Nearctic up the ramp of the Windfields horse trailer and set out for Nearctic's first race. An hour later the van rolled to a halt in the backstretch of the Old Woodbine track.

Pete chose to begin Nearctic in a 4-1/2-furlong dash for maiden two-year-olds. With jockey Vic Bovine along for the ride, Nearctic let the world know how *he* liked to win races. At the sound of the bell, Nearctic bounded out of the gate and immediately went to the head of the pack. If Nearctic thought the rest of the horses were trying to chase him down, he ensured they would never catch him. With every stride, the distance between Nearctic and the others grew wider.

"The first time he raced," recalled Bill Reeves, "zoom! He was out front—six, seven lengths in front...Then Vic Bovine reached back and hit Nearctic two times. The Irish in Pete went through the roof. He was furious!

"After the race Pete went up to him and said 'What did you hit him for?' and Bovine said, 'He wasn't paying attention. He was looking over at the stands.'

"'Well you won't ever be riding this horse again,' Pete told him.

"Pete didn't believe in hitting a horse that was well in the lead. He'd tell the jockey just to hand-ride the horse. He sure didn't want anyone hitting Nearctic. He was really mad."

The headline in the *Daily Racing Form* read: "Nearctic Easy Winner in First Start." On the front page, next to the Nearctic story was a brief item under the headline: "Aussie Ace Rae Johnstone Wins Guineas On Pederoba." On the day that Nearctic won his first horse race, jockey Rae Johnstone won his twenty-ninth European Classic, the Irish One Thousand Guineas, at The Curragh. Several years later, and under curious circumstances, Nearctic, the Canadian-foaled colt conceived in Great Britain, and Rae Johnstone, the Australian-born jockey making his mark in Europe, would come together—in California.

Nearctic was entered in his second 4-1/2-furlong race, this one written for non-winners of two races. It was the fifth race of the afternoon; Nearctic was carrying jockey George Walker.

In this, Nearctic's second race, yet another pattern began— Nearctic would have ten different jockeys, thirteen if you count his exercise riders—two of whom were retired jockeys and the third, a vacationing jockey. Nearctic's list of jockeys was even longer than that of his most famous son, Northern Dancer. Northern Dancer's seven different jockeys was outrageous.

It is considered to be in the best interests of a horse to match it with a rider who is compatible with its disposition and capabilities. This is particularly critical for horses campaigning in the major stakes races, where the competition is intense and victory is measured in fractions.

According to the *Daily Racing Form*: "Nearctic assumed command soon after the start. Steadily came away from his opposition and won with something in reserve." Nearctic won by three lengths.

Nearctic's third race was the Swansea Plate, a five furlong stake for two-year-olds at Taylor's brand new Woodbine Park. The gigantic state-of-the-art horse-racing facility had been open only two weeks. For this, his first outing on his owner's new track, Nearctic was carrying jockey Avelino Gomez and top weight of 122 pounds.

Nearctic jumped sharply out of the gate and off he went. Early in the home stretch he was at least six lengths ahead of the rest. Gomez sat relaxed, his face inches from Nearctic's flying mane, and simply hand-rode the colt as they soared past the finish.

Nearctic won the Swansea Plate by an astounding ten lengths!

"Gomez should have paid us for the privilege of riding Nearctic that day," laughed Bill Reeves.

Nearctic was entered in the five-furlong Claredon Stakes at Woodbine Park with Avelino Gomez back in the saddle. The combination of Nearctic and Gomez was a good one, but interesting. Both horse and jockey were talented, volatile and head-strong. Both appeared to have an over-abundance of nervous energy. Perhaps because of this, they understood each other. In this, their second encounter, Nearctic won by 9-1/2 lengths! The huge margin is especially remarkable considering the relatively short distance raced.

Nearctic repeated his winning pattern: he took command instantly and drew farther away from the other horses. And once again, Gomez simply hand-rode Nearctic. There could be little doubt that Nearctic outclassed all the other horses.

Nearctic's fifth two-year-old start was the five-and-a-half-furlong Victoria Stakes. Again his partner was Avelino Gomez. This was Nearctic's toughest challenge to date. He bounded out of the gate and quickly established considerable airspace between him and the rest of the pack. This time, however, the top two-year-old colt, Mr. Jive, was sent in heated pursuit of Nearctic. (One of the top horses of his generation, Mr. Jive would finish seventh in the 1957 Kentucky Derby behind such outstanding horses, as Gallant Man, Bold Ruler and Round Table.)

After the first quarter Mr. Jive was closing in on the charging Nearctic, but during the stretch run, and despite the sting of his jockey's stick, Mr. Jive was unable to catch Nearctic. Mr. Jive crossed the finish two-and-a-half lengths behind the winner.

"This was an important race," mused Bill Reeves, more than forty years later. "Until now, Nearctic had no real competition. This was the first time he had ever been challenged, and he answered the challenge."

Pete McCann's fastidious care of this horse—riding Nearctic every morning, understanding and quelling Nearctic's demons—built the foundation for Nearctic's transition from a handsome, beautifully-bred horse, to a racehorse.

Nearctic's full brother, Empire Day, was entered in the 1956 Toronto Cup Handicap, which followed Nearctic's win in the Victoria Stakes. (Empire Day was Lady Angela's frightened little foal that Harry Green got off the ship from England in the summer of 1953.) According to the *Daily Racing Form* chart, "Empire Day showed great speed in the first half and then faltered." Ridden by Vic Bovine, Empire Day was leading the pack by a length at the half-mile pole in this mile-and-a-sixteenth excursion, but, unlike his brother, he was unable to maintain the speed. The winner was Winifred Taylor's Censor, a son of Bull Page. Avelino Gomez was the winning jockey.

A month earlier, on 14 June 1956, Avelino Gomez had teamed up with Empire Day in the Belle Mahone Purse for "non-winners of $1470 twice other than maiden or claiming." And he won clearly, by a length. According to the *Daily Racing Form*, "Empire Day assumed command soon after the start. Raced a trifle wide entering the stretch, and responded gamely when roused during the drive."

Empire Day was not entered in the Queen's Plate, to be run two days later, because he was foaled in England; the Queen's Plate is restricted to Thoroughbreds foaled in Canada.

The Plate was won by Canadian Champ, the striking-looking son of Windfields that Bill Beasley had purchased at Taylor's inaugural yearling sale. London Calling, one of the Windfields horses that had not been purchased that year and now running in Taylor's name, finished third in the race. Winifred Taylor's Censor was fourth. In sixth place was Bunty's Flight, a son of the great Bunty Lawless. (Bunty's Flight is the sire of Mint Copy, dam of two-time leading North American stallion, Deputy Minister.)

After the 1956 Queen's Plate, on 5 July, Bunty's Flight won the six-and-one-half furlong Dundurn Plate at Woodbine Park. Empire Day galloped across the finish tenth in a field of eleven.

Four days later, Bunty's Flight and Empire Day were back in the same starting gate, for the mile-and-seventy-yard Irving Goshen Purse. With Avelino Gomez in the saddle, Empire Day forced the early pace but could not fend off Bunty's Flight.

"He [Empire Day] was a grand looking colt," recalled Bill Reeves. "A chestnut, like his mother."

Empire Day started in twelve races in 1956. He won two, was second once, and third four times, one of that very large herd of beautifully-bred Thoroughbreds by Nearco and out of daughters of Hyperion that did not excel as racehorses.

While Empire Day was not deemed to be a racehorse, by the middle of July 1956, two-year-old Nearctic had started five times, and won five times, twice by huge margins.

Yet, at this point someone decided that Nearctic should go to the United States to race. More precisely, to Saratoga.

The Saratoga race meet in August was the height of Thoroughbred racing's social season. Everyone who was anyone in the North American horse racing circles was there, including Edward and Winifred Taylor. They would fly to Saratoga while their chauffeur drove the Taylor's limousine to the famed spa, so that he could ferry them from the house they rented for the season to the races, horse sales and parties.

No doubt pleased with Nearctic's performances, Taylor may have wished to have his regally-bred colt perform before his friends, associates and the rest of the racing crowd at Saratoga. The problem was that Nearctic's trainer, Pete McCann, did not want to go to along.

One reason was that Pete had a huge string of Windfields horses to look after—between the yearlings on the farm and the racehorses at the track, he was responsible for more than fifty horses. Pete was part horse. He understood the need for consistency. And his commitment to these horses was enormous.

"He basically lived with the horses under his care," explained Bill Reeves. "He arrived in the backstretch every morning at 3:30 sharp. He was the first person on the shedrow. He checked every horse."

Pete liked to get his horses out and exercised very early in the morning, so he wanted their morning meal to be well digested before he began exercising them.

The second reason that he didn't want to go to Saratoga was that he did not like to go anywhere. Ever. The man was painfully shy. The stories of Pete McCann's reticence are legend.

"Heck, it was hard to get Pete to cross the road," laughed Bill Reeves, "He thought Fort Erie was a long way, and that's what, an hour and a half from Toronto. Horses were his life, horses and his family. I think the only place he went willingly, other than to the farm or the track, was to watch his daughters play baseball. Two of his daughters were good ball players — Joyce and Reta. He was really proud of them."

That Pete, could not or would not go to Saratoga turned out to be a serious problem, especially for the horse. Moreover, Nearctic's jockey, Avelino Gomez, was not permitted to ride in the United States.

"It's close and fast. It's wit and nerves. You breathe the sweat of the horses and you taste the track. You got to find your position by a few feet and try not to get bumped. To hug the rail from start to finish is the fastest route, but not everyone can travel on the inside. Who is outside? Who is inside? Where is a gap going to open up? You got to think in split seconds."

AVELINO GOMEZ

Avelino Gomez was unable to go to the United States to ride Nearctic because U.S. federal authorities considered him a draft dodger. The Cuban-born jockey was riding in Chicago in 1951 and had registered for the draft; but when it looked as if he might be called upon to fight in the Korean war, the twenty-two-year-old left for home.

"Uncle Sam's complaint against me was that when I was called up for army duty I didn't report," explained Gomez many years later. "When my name came up, I wasn't there. I was in Cuba and content to stay there."

With a thick mop of curly black hair, flashing brown eyes and leathery mobile features, Avelino Gomez strutted with the swagger of a champion. The media labelled him "El Perfecto" or "El Senor." Flashy, fiery, charming and glib, Gomez had a colourful and frequently funny response for every situation.

The racetrack was his stage, for both his innate ability with horses and his antics. Gomez was not only a brilliant jockey, but, for years he ruled as the clown prince of horse racing.

The fans called him Gomey. They either loved him, or loved to hate him. They heckled him when he won. They heckled him when he lost. Gomez responded by sticking out his tongue or raising his middle finger at the crowds in the grandstand all in good fun. And Gomez revelled in reactions he provoked.

One afternoon Gomez and his mount were flying down the track on what appeared to be an easy victory, when, several hundred yards from the finish, his horse stumbled and fell. Gomez was catapulted out of the saddle and into the path of the charging field. Miraculously, he managed to roll under the infield fence and out of harm's way. After the horses galloped past, Gomez stood up, brushed himself off, and waved to the crowd. The fans cheered with relief. However, as he crossed the dirt track in front of the grandstand, the booing began. The closer he got, the more intense the heckling.

So he stopped, bowed to the crowds and said, in his thick Spanish accent, "Maybe next time I kill myself."

Avelino Gomez understood show biz. He understood the drama, the irony, the foolishness. He also understood horse racing, the horses, the fans. Where else can you become instantly part of an event, without knowing anything about the sport?

It seems so simple, and so beautiful. It begins with a pageant— a parade of magnificent animals. You choose your favourite—your favourite number, your favourite colour. You back your hunch. The starting bell clangs and you jump up and down and scream your lungs out. And you get to do it all ten times on any afternoon at the racetrack. In the days of Avelino Gomez, fans also got a bonus— they could yell at him too.

"Baseball was nothing without Babe Ruth; horse racing's nothing without Avelino Gomez," he was fond of saying.

When he won a race he leapt for joy, bounding high above the saddle and landing squarely on his feet next to the horse, a huge grin stretched across his weathered face:

"That's the Gomez trademark, the Gomez style," he would explain, a style that would be copied by other jockeys, some more successfully than others.

Born in 1929 in Havana, Avelino was one of five children of a city cab driver. By the time he was twelve Avelino was working in a casino; and later graduated to bellhop at the Havana Jockey Club. He was small and wiry, and before long people were telling him he should be a jockey.

"I became a jockey by accident," he explained. "I didn't know nothing about horses, but I get a job in the barns and after two years I start galloping horses."

Avelino Gomez rode his first winner in Mexico City in 1944. The following year, the 16 year-old migrated to Vancouver. He soon became the leading rider at Hastings Park, but was suspended for allegedly cheating.

"One day a friend of mine called Gonzales came to me and asked for help. He was broke and he needed to win a race. I was on the favourite, Ascot Maid, in the race where his horse was running and he wanted me to pull her.

"There was no talk of money. I was just doing him a favour. Well, the stewards saw what was going on."

This would not have been difficult, for Ascot Maid seemed bent on winning. And there was her jockey tugging away at the rein trying to slow her down.

"The stewards declared the race no contest, and they told me to pack my gear and go home and don't bother coming back."

"I went home to Havana and rode there. And then two years later the same people in Vancouver gave me the biggest boost of my life. They decided I was older and wiser and they licenced me. That was the real start of my career in North America."

After riding in Vancouver for a season, Gomez drifted to the United States. He was riding in Chicago when it appeared that he might well be drafted, so he returned to Cuba.

In 1955 a friend asked if he would consider coming back to Canada. For the next three years Gomez was the leading Canadian jockey. In 1958 he was back in Cuba to invest his earnings in an apartment complex and bar, which he called The Toronto Club. When Fidel Castro took over, Avelino Gomez, entrepreneur, left the country. Broke. So he returned to Canada and to being Avelino Gomez, champion jockey.

Gomez's charisma belied his innate toughness. His philosophy was simple: "You let somebody step on you, you might as well stay at home and wash dishes." He was also volatile. His fiery disposition landed him countless suspensions and fines. Once he and jockey Hugo Dittfach were in a fist fight; Gomez ended up with a black eye. Gomez shrugged the whole thing off as part of the business.

"Nobody holds grudges," laughed Gomez the following day.

But he desperately wanted to ride in the United States, where horse racing was conducted on a much grander scale. The money was better; but more important, he wanted to prove himself. "I had achieved certain things and I was proud of them, but I wanted more. I always believed that I could ride against the best big-league jockeys — Ycaza, Shoemaker, Hartack, guys like that—and win my share."

His other incentive was that his wife, Patricia, was from Buffalo, New York. They had two children and his wife wanted to raise them in the States. Finally, their wish came true.

"My wife's family persuaded some political men from the Buffalo area to help, and in 1961 they gave me a visa which says there's no limit on how long I can stay. Since then, I received documents saying the matter of my draft evasion was closed. I was forgiven. I felt so sure everything was going to be fine, I bought a $30,000 house in Hollywood, Florida, and the Gomez family settled down."

Gomez's euphoria was short-lived. Early in 1964 United States government agents arrived at the door with papers demanding that Gomez leave the United States by 17 February 1964. After that date he would be escorted out of the country:

"I tried and I tried to find out the reason for this sudden switch, and the only thing I can learn is that I said something wrong to the U.S. ambassador in Havana many years ago. Anyway, I decided to give up and quit fighting. I am sick of losing out to governments. Mr. Castro took away my bar and apartment buildings in Havana. Now this.

"They don't like the way I talk and maybe tomorrow they'll decide they don't like the way I comb my hair or that I should shave off my moustache. I don't want to stay where people don't want me and I won't try to stay."

And Gomez returned to Canada, where he was wanted and certainly appreciated. E.P. Taylor put it succinctly, "Mr. Gomez is undoubtedly one of the world's great jockeys."

"Avelino was an inspiration to us younger jocks," said champion Sandy Hawley. "He was a super rider, quick-witted, and rode over 4,000 winners. And he was fun to be around. If you were feeling down, he'd pick you up in no time."

It seems that Gomez was born to ride. He had good hands, razor-sharp instincts and an innate sense of how much his horse had to give at any point in any race.

"He just seems to be able to get more run out of a horse than anybody else," said Bruce Walker, former Ontario Jockey Club publicity director.

"One of the reasons Gomez was so successful," adds Bill Reeves, "was his ability to bring his horse out of the gate straight and fast. You check the charts. He was always one, two or three out of the gate. He'd have the horse ready.

"Also, Gomez had a real razzle-dazzle style, when it came to using his whip. You'd hear a lot of slap, slap, slap. But he never hurt them, not that I ever saw. I'd check our horses after every race. There was never a mark."

But in 1956, Avelino Gomez was still considered a draft dodger in the United States and not allowed to ride Nearctic in his U.S. races.

This was a great pity, because Avelino Gomez *knew* the horse.

This story might have been quite different had Gomez—or a top U.S. rider—been in the saddle. But the question lingers: Why didn't they hire a top U.S. jockey and stick with him whenever Nearctic was raced in the United States?

Near the end of July, racing stables across the United States prepare for their annual migration to Saratoga, the most picturesque and charming racetrack in North America. Nestled in the foothills of the Catskill mountains in upper New York State, Saratoga Springs is a quaint village of gingerbread Victorian homes, broad avenues and giant elm trees. The August race meet at Saratoga is a glimpse back to a time when some of America's most famous, and infamous, citizens flocked here to enjoy the spas, mineral waters, parties, gambling and horse racing, a time of great opulence and greater decadence.

Saratoga's colourful history can be traced to an Irish brawler named John Morrisey. Nicknamed Old Smoke, Morrisey had been a New York gang leader, a bouncer in brothels, a hired thug, an election-fixer, and eventually, a United States Congressman. Morrisey was thirty when he arrived in Saratoga, and soon opened the town's first big-time gambling hall. Two years later he built a racetrack. When it proved to be too small, he built a larger, grander one, where Saratoga racetrack now stands.

The first official race meet was conducted there in August 1863, less than a month after the Battle of Gettysburg. The event lasted only three days and attracted only forty-five Thoroughbreds, but was considered a resounding success. The *Spirit of the Times*, a weekly sporting newspaper, described the event as "... where the elegance and superb costumes of the ladies vie with the blood and beauty of the running horses." And so it has been every August since.

Through into the early 1900s the streets were full of great characters. Actress Lillian Russell would be seen riding around town on her gold-plated bicycle, her name set in diamonds — a gift from her boyfriend, the flamboyant gambler, (Diamond) Jim Brady. Horse owner John Payne Whitney and his son William could be found on the tennis courts playing for $10,000 a set, or on the polo field playing for even higher stakes.

Then there was John (Bet a Million) Gates. One afternoon, after losing $400,000 at the track, he went directly to the Canfield Casino, where he lost another $150,000. He continued gambling all night long and by daybreak he had won most of his money back. These all-night gambling binges were the norm for many Saratoga visitors, and were generally followed by a champagne breakfast at the race track.

Saratoga's gambling culture changed in 1939, when the bookmakers were replaced by pari-mutuel machines. Eleven years later the Kefauver hearings made the casino's gaming tables and roulette wheels illegal. The one tradition that remained, however, was horse racing; during August each year, Saratoga hosts some of the most presitgious stakes races on the continent.

■ 6 AUGUST 1956. SARATOGA SPRINGS, NEW YORK

On opening day at Saratoga, Nearctic was entered in the 82nd running of The Flash Stakes, a five-and-a-half-furlong allowance race. Nearctic had been given to U.S. trainer, C.W. (Charley) Shaw, to prepare the colt for the Saratoga races. There is no record of who hired Shaw, or why he was chosen for the task. Nearctic was to be ridden by, Eric Guerin, the U.S. jockey familiar to millions from his frequent trips to the winner's circle aboard Native Dancer. Televised coverage of major North America horse races had coincided with the career of Native Dancer, and the grand grey colt became a television star and public idol. Viewers saw his jockey, Guerin, smiling happily, time after time, for the cameras.

Four years earlier, Guerin had ridden Native Dancer to victory in Flash Stakes at Saratoga, in Native Dancer's second stakes victory.

For the 1956 running, according to the *Daily Racing Form*; "the crowd was swelled considerably by the Canadians who came down to see E.P. Taylor's unbeaten Nearctic in his U.S. debut."

Nearctic's Canadian fans at Saratoga were apparently more enthused about Nearctic than was his new trainer, Charley Shaw, the *Form* columnist added. "Before the race, Charley Shaw, trainer of Nearctic, said that if the colt didn't prove himself in the Flash he would be promptly returned to Toronto, adding that he would have no alibis."

At the sound of the bell, Nearctic flew out of the gate, determined to take the immediate lead, as usual. Eric Guerin, however, held the anxious colt in second place, running neck and neck with a horse called Willing Worker.

"Nearctic was used up vying for the lead."reported the *Daily Racing Form*, and Nearctic finished eighth.

"You don't fight a horse like Nearctic," offered Bill Reeves. "You shouldn't have to fight any of them, but Nearctic was a big free-running horse. He had *his* particular way. The more you fight a horse like Nearctic, the more he fights back. The energy you waste fighting, is the energy the horse needs to win the race."

Among the Canadians in attendance on that gloomy Saratoga afternoon was Pete McCann. If he was unwilling, or unable to take the time away from the other Windfields horses, to train Nearctic for U.S. races, Taylor had insisted that he at least come to Saratoga on the day of the race. Pete's travelling companion on the ten-hour drive from Toronto was a thirty-two year old American, Joe Thomas.

The previous summer Taylor had been in Kentucky for the July yearling sales. One evening at dinner he was telling the story of how he had ended up with two farms, and therefore, too many horses, and how this had led to his pre-priced yearling sale. What he needed now was to find someone who could take over the paper work involved. The person would also prepare the yearling sale catalogue and deal with advertising and publicity. (Taylor had asked his godson, television journalist and horse-racing afficionado, Michael Magee, but he declined.)

One of the dinner guests, Ellen Carruthers, suggested Joe Thomas. Warner Jones, president of Churchill Downs, concurred.

The story goes that Thomas had arrived in Lexington from California in February 1951 in a boxcar with half a dozen yearlings. The horses, which belonged to John D. Hertz, and their groom, Joe Thomas, were headed for local horse dealer and publicist, John (Trader) Clark.

The day the freight train rattled into town, the horse racing columnist for the Lexington *Herald* dropped dead. Clark was then publicity director at Keeneland, and knew the importance of favourable media coverage. The vacancy at the *Herald* needed to be filled quickly, and by someone inclined to give Clark favourable coverage. The person best qualified for the job was Clark himself, but that might have seemed a tad obvious. So, he wrote the column and said it was by a young fellow just come from California, named Joe Thomas. If pressed, Trader Clark could have assured the Herald sports editor that Thomas had done some writing in California. Thomas had written one story, about a horse called Eight Thirty. There is no record of the story being published.

During the next few weeks Clark wrote the column under the Joe Thomas byline, while training his protégé to write the column on his own. (Clark also had Thomas mucking out stalls and researching pedigrees.) After several weeks, Clark handed over the column to Thomas.

Thomas continued working for Clark, doing the *Herald* column and compiling stallion and farm directories for the *Daily Racing Form*. In 1956, Thomas was, once again, in the right place at the right time. E.P. Taylor was about to become the world's leading breeder of Thoroughbreds and he invited Thomas to join the Windfields team.

According to Taylor: "Thomas will be on the paper side of the business. With so many horses ... I had to have more help, and Thomas is the man to do the job. Just mention a horse and he'll tell you the pedigree right back to the tree."

Thomas's interest in pedigrees and statistical information had begun when he was quite young. His sister contracted scarlet fever, and the family lived in quarantine for several months. With little to occupy them, Joe and his older brother made a game of checking the newspaper for the entries at the local track and handicapping the races. They kept scrapbooks on their selections and how they fared. When the quarantine was lifted, the two boys apparently continued their handicapping. Every afternoon they visited Santa Anita to find an adult to place their wagers.

Thomas's first job was delivering tout sheets and running the occasional wager for housewives. Next he worked for a pharmacist who doubled as a bookie. Later he worked as a hot walker for B.R. (Bankroll) Roberts, before serving two stints in the U.S. navy. He sold insurance, briefly, before ending up in Lexington.

One of Thomas's tasks was to speak to the news media. Taylor understood the value of good press, but to suggest that Taylor disliked being interviewed was a vast understatement.

(When I set out, a rookie reporter, in 1968 to do a story on Taylor, it took me eight months to get an interview with him. My extreme naiveté helped, and luck played a major role, and even then, I know it would not have taken place without the sanction of Taylor's assistant, Beth Heriot who, no doubt, had tired of having me turn up at Taylor's office every few days.)

It is not clear what Joe Thomas's title was, but it wasn't long before he had bounced from doing the paper side of the business, to racing manager. Not unlike his foray into newspaper writing, it was a position for which he was severely underqualified.

He had walked hots and mucked out stalls. In 1947 he and his new wife joined his brother on a ten-acre farm and apparently set out to breed racehorses. The scheme was short-lived. Thomas reenlisted in the navy and was posted in Hawaii for a year-and-a-half. When he returned to California he resumed his career as a groom, which is when he became acquainted with John (Trader) Clark. Thomas had neither run a racing stable, nor trained a horse.

Perhaps because Thomas knew nothing about training horses, he seemed unable to discern Pete McCann's ability with horses, nor his extraordinary value to Windfields Farm. For once Thomas assumed the title of *racing manager*, he declared that he, not Pete McCann, was in charge of the Windfields racing stable. Before long, Thomas could be spotted in the walking ring, prior to a race, giving instructions to the jockey.

It was never difficult to spot Thomas. He was a tall man and appeared even taller by the array of hats he took to wearing. The collection included everything from boaters to bowlers. Suffice to say, Joe Thomas stood out in a crowd.

Pete McCann, by contrast, was practically invisible, the antithesis of Thomas. Thomas spoke an ersatz Kentucky drawl that could be heard from some distance; Pete barely spoke at all. Thomas was comfortable at the centre of a media scrum or among the owners and OJC directors during the festivities in the Trustee's rooms after a Windfields horse won a big race. Pete fairly blanched at the prospect and consistently refused to attend. He didn't even want to go to the annual party at Windfields after the Queen's Plate, not even after one of the horses he trained had won—which happened frequently.

"I remember one year," recalled McCann's daughter, Reta. "A Windfields horse had won —New Providence, I think. Dad had gone to the party, but I guess as soon as nobody was looking, he came home. He just had changed out of his suit and there was a knock at the door. It was Bill Reeves. Mr. Taylor had sent him to bring Dad back to the party."

Pete McCann was gifted and diffident; but he was also a very stubborn man. So it wasn't long before the acrimony between McCann and Joe Thomas began to set in.

Nonetheless, following the 1956 Flash Stakes, Pete McCann and Joe Thomas drove through the night to arrive at the Fort Erie racetrack early the following morning. Rather than explain that jockey Guerin had mishandled or misjudged the race, or that trainer, Charley Shaw's instructions to the jockey might have led him to mishandle or misjudge the race, Thomas announced to the reporters: "Nearctic did not extend himself at any stage. He may not have liked the deep footing."

Contrary to trainer Charley Shaw's prediction that Nearctic would promptly return to Toronto should he not prove himself in the Flash Stakes, Nearctic remained in Saratoga.

■ **13 AUGUST 1956. SARATOGA SPRINGS, NEW YORK**

The day dawned cloudy and rainy for the 54th running of the six-furlong Saratoga Special Stakes. U.S.-born jockey, George Walker, who had ridden Nearctic in the colt's second race several months earlier, was brought to New York for the Saratoga Special Stakes.

This time Nearctic was allowed to run as he wished, at least for the first part of the race. He broke on top and led the entire distance:

13 AUGUST 1956. SARATOGA SPRINGS, NEW YORK

"Clever Canadian-bred Outruns Crack Rivals On Muddy Course," reported the *Daily Racing Form*. "Bounding back from his only defeat in the Flash Stakes, Canadian-foaled Nearctic led throughout the winner-take-all Saratoga Special today.

"Nearctic displayed high speed from the outside. Raced well away from the rail in better going and was hard ridden to turn back Clem who chased Nearctic the entire way. At the half Nearctic was leading by seven lengths. At the finish he won by three-quarters of a length."

Nearctic won, but further analysis of that win revealed some disturbing information. The first, was noticed by the *Daily Racing Form*. "Making a wide arc into the stretch, his lead was cut to four lengths and George Walker struck him alongside the head, once hitting him in the eye trying to keep him in."

Horses will try to "run out" or try to escape from the race for a number of reasons. Perhaps the horse has not experienced balanced or good training. But if the animal has been reasonably trained, running out generally indicates that the horse has a physical ailment.

Nearctic ran to form: He went to the lead, and he stayed there. He did not try to run from the competition; he was not a compliant animal.

Nearctic was running wide in the Saratoga Special because he was suffering bucked shins, an inflamation of the metacarpal (cannon) bone of the forelegs. The condition is caused by undue stress and most susceptible are young racehorses in training. The symptoms are obvious: lameness, usually in both forelegs, but it may be more pronounced in one leg than the other; swelling on the front of the canon bone, which if not caught immediately, thickens in a convex shape. It is very painful. The main treatment is rest, along with warm applications of anti-inflammatory treatments such as antiphlogistine, soaking frequently in tepid water and light bandaging.

According to the *Daily Racing Form*, Nearctic's handlers were aware of his condition; "but it was hoped to run him once more before stopping him, so he appeared for the [Saratoga] Special."

■ **1 SEPTEMBER 1956. SARATOGA SPRINGS, NEW YORK**

Clear and sunny skies heralded this, the final day of the 1956 Saratoga summer race meeting. Nearctic was entered in the 52nd running of the six-and-a-half-furlong Hopeful Stakes. George Walker was in the saddle, and again, Nearctic went straight for the lead. At the half Nearctic was leading by four lengths, but coming into the stretch, leading U.S. jockey, Eddie Arcaro, set King Hairan in hot pursuit at a blistering pace. The sensation of the east coast winter season, King Hairan wore down Nearctic, who began to tire and drift out. King Hairan overtook Nearctic in the stretch and won the race. Nearctic was fourth.

This should not have been a great surprise: only a fortnight earlier Nearctic had gone into the Saratoga Special Stakes with bucked shins. Jockey George Walker beating him on the head and in the eye in that race, no doubt created greater stress and inflamation.

"When their shins are like that, they are hot and the pain is biting," Bill Reeves explained. "There was no way Nearctic was going to run to form in that kind of pain."

Following the Hopeful Stakes, Nearctic was shipped home to Windfields Farm.

And yet another pattern was established: When things looked hopeless, Nearctic was returned to the care of Pete McCann; when Nearctic's health had been restored, Nearctic was removed from McCann.

■ **22 SEPTEMBER 1956. OLD WOODBINE RACECOURSE**

For the first running of the six-furlong Carleton Stakes, Nearctic was back among old friends. When he arrived back from Saratoga, sore and extremely anxious, Nearctic received a well-deserved rest on the farm, but McCann did continue working with the colt.

Before long, Nearctic had settled down considerably under McCann's constant care and McCann resumed his exercise program—riding in the mornings, training, and both mental and physical conditioning.

McCann contracted Avelino Gomez to ride Nearctic in the upcoming races, a winning combination.

The second the bell signalled the start of the Carleton Stakes, Nearctic blasted to the front of the pack and galloped off into an authoritative lead. He led the field the entire distance and won the Carleton Stakes by 4-1/2 lengths.

However, after the race, Nearctic was showing signs of a quarter crack in his left front hoof, the same stress-related injury that would sideline his son, Northern Dancer. (Technical advances in treating quarter cracks allowed Northern Dancer to resume training and racing, but in Nearctic's day, time was the only healer.)

Unfortunately Nearctic was not given that time.

A quarter crack appears as a vertical split in the wall of the hoof, just below the coronet, the band at the top of the hoof. The exterior of the hoof grows downward from the coronet and is comprised of thousands of tiny tubes bound together. The coronet houses papillae, projections that connect to the upper end of each tube, through which secretions necessary for growth travel. If an injury occurs to the papillae, secretion is interrupted and growth in that area of the hoof stops.

There is a saying: "No foot, no horse." And that is the result if an injury to the hoof is not looked after immediately, for a problem in one foot soon throws the biomechanics of the entire horse out of kilter.

Following the sighting of the quarter crack Nearctic was not given time out in order for the hoof to repair. Instead Nearctic was shipped back to Charley Shaw, at Belmont Park, to be prepared for the Anticipation Purse, and two weeks later, the Belmont Futurity.

That Nearctic was able to endure this colossal incompetence is remarkable. It does, however, indicate how tough Nearctic must have been: from this point to the end of the year, he was essentially running on three feet, and in pain and stress.

That they continued racing Nearctic does not reflect well on Windfields Farm, and poses the question: Where was E.P. Taylor in all this? The E.P. Taylor I knew cared about his horses. Beth Heriot talked about the time she found him sitting at his desk weeping. He had just been told that the mare Nandi, dam of Windfields, had died.

One of my favourite images of E.P. Taylor was the time I entered the stable and saw him in the stall with his arms wrapped around the neck of his riding horse. He was talking to the horse. And patting it. It seemed so touching that I exited the barn as quickly and quietly as I could.

"I honestly don't believe Mr. Taylor would have run Nearctic if he had known the horse was lame," said Beth Heriot. "And Pete certainly wouldn't."

E.P. Taylor was a brilliant entrepreneur. He was charming, clever, charismatic and essentially unflappable. And when it came to the game of business, he was Grand Master: He wrote the rules; changed the rules; and delighted in every stage—from conception to fruition.

But once Taylor got an enterprise up and running, he handed over the reins. He had no interest in the drudgery of running any one business. While he felt that if he had stuck to one enterprise he would have fared better financially, he preferred taking risks, facing challenges, and he liked variety.

"A lot of people don't understand why I spread myself among eight or ten businesses." Taylor explained. "It's because I always felt I could find somebody who could run a business on a day-to-day basis better than myself."

"All through my life I have had great satisfaction in holding something together and improving it in bad times. Then I lose interest when the times are good."

E.P. Taylor was a restless man—always going somewhere; building something; negotiating; creating. When I lived and worked on Windfields estate, I had the impression that if he stopped, he would expire—as if fueled by this perpetual motion. Even when he was relaxing, he was deep in thought. His mind seemed to work on many tracks at one time.

Once when we were riding around the estate, he was telling me his plans to revise horse racing in Quebec. Suddenly his horse shied and I caught a glimpse of astonishment in his eyes as he began to tumble earthward. I realized at that moment that he was so engrossed in his racing scheme, that he had forgotten he was on the back of a horse.

On another occasion he was behind the wheel of one of the Windfields station wagons, a rare event, since he was usually driven by a chauffeur and therefore didn't have pay attention. We had been to visit Nearctic and when we departed he set the gear shift handle on R, for reverse, rather than D, for drive, then stepped on the gas; and off we went—bam, right into the side of Mrs. du Pont's barn. Again, he simply forgot what he was doing.

When he was young, his fraternity brothers made a game of passing him salt when he asked for sugar and then laughed uproariously as he not only stirred the salt into his tea, but drank it without noticing. A Delta Upsilon Fraternity verse of 1921 describes Taylor:

"If he's often absent-minded why should that be called a fault?
For he gives his friends enjoyment when he fills his tea with salt.
When the finance of a nation is being settled in his head
Is it strange that Ed would pass a spoon when asked for

bread?

… But laugh you simple brothers, laugh your loudest one and all…

Our Edward will have millions, clever Edward, lucky Ed."

So where was Taylor during the time of Nearctic? The simple answer: taking care of business; creating those millions that ultimately financed his one great hobby—horses.

By the 1950s Taylor's initial foray into the brewery business had grown into a major corporation, Canadian Breweries—which was now part of his holding company, Argus Corporation. Other companies in the Argus conglomerate included Standard Broadcasting, Dominion Stores, Dominion Tar and Chemical, Hollinger Gold Mines, Massey Ferguson Limited, Noranda Mines and B.C Forest Products.

He was also revamping Canadian horse racing, buying up all the small Ontario racetracks, converting their racing charters, and building Woodbine, his super track, which opened in 1956.

In 1952 he bought 600-acre Donalda Farm, giving him a total of 2200 acres in the north-east end of Toronto. On this land he built a golf and country club and the suburb of Don Mills. Unique, then and now, Don Mills continues to be studied by urban planners: "I decided that Don Mills must not look like a lot of places I had seen around the world where you see 500 or 1,000 houses that all look alike close together."

Also in 1952 Taylor spear-headed a campaign to raise money for the Toronto General Hospital. Almost every day for six months Taylor worked relentlessly; he and his team, which included the city's most prominent business leaders, raised more than $2 million beyond their target. That same year he agreed to assist the Victorian Order of Nurses with their fund-raising. And several years later, when the Art Gallery of Ontario needed money, the board invited Taylor to help out, and he did.

In 1954 he purchased 2,800 acres on the island of New Providence in the Bahamas. In 1956 he began construction of the Lyford Cay Club. The property started as a mangrove swamp, and ended up as the most exclusive resort anywhere, at the time. The evolution from swamp to club could only have happened under the guidance of someone as cheerfully determined as Taylor. The project did, however, consume considerable time and energy.

In 1955 Taylor announced his intention to build a theatre for the performing arts in Toronto and name it O'Keefe, after one of his brands of beer. "This wasn't all charity or philanthropy," explained Taylor. "To be perfectly honest, one of the reasons behind building the O'Keefe Centre was to sell beer. But we wanted to do something for all Ontario. We thought it was a goodwill gesture."

The 3,200 seat O'Keefe Centre opened October 1960 with the musical *Camelot*. Richard Burton played King Arthur and Julie Andrews was Queen Guinevere.

In 1957, when the Bank of Canada had outgrown its premises at 10 Toronto Street, the government announced the building was to be demolished after the bank moved to a new facility. Built in 1852, the building was considered a valuable historic site, and there was a great public outcry. So Taylor and his partners bought the building, restored it to its original splendour, and established it as headquarters for Argus Corp.

"Four Toronto financiers [gave] Toronto a Christmas present for which every citizen can be grateful," reported the Toronto *Telegram*. "They have saved for the city its finest piece of architecture—the Bank of Canada building on Toronto Street, which faced demolition next year."

As if he had nothing else to occupy his days, during the 1950s Taylor embarked upon another project, one not dissimilar to his Ontario brewery mergers in the 1930s. Taylor set his sights on Great Britain's brewing industry and began travelling around England and Scotland investigating and purchasing breweries. By 1960 his company, United Breweries, had amassed more than 1,500 public houses in Yorkshire and Scotland.

It did not make him entirely popular: when two major British breweries merged, the *Daily Telegraph* crowed: "the move shuts one more door for Mr. E.P. Taylor, Canadian head of United Breweries, who had been energetically pushing his way into the British brewing industry."

In response, Devon Smith, financial editor of the Toronto *Telegram* wrote an interesting essay on Taylor:

> "E.P. is having trouble with his shadow. He's finding that its size throws people into a panic. Not too many years ago, E.P. was known, trusted and liked by a very large number of unimportant people. He was recognized as honest, good-natured, friendly and superbly confident. A big man physically, he had a friendly twinkle in his eye and a thoughtful—sometimes grim—expression, though the ability to smile or laugh heartily was always pretty well in evidence. And he had infinite patience with people who depended upon him...
>
> "E.P. seemed to disappear as his shadow grew. Once in awhile, you'd hear a friendly voice say, "Hello there!" and you'd spot the half-forgotten twinkle behind a cloud of smoke from E.P.'s ever-present pipe. But those occasions have become mighty rare. E.P. very definitely had become one of those persons who are known of, but not known."

E.P. Taylor did cast an enormous shadow, it was almost palpable, but he never lost his cheerfulness, his curiosity, or his common touch. It simply became obscured by the growing number of people he delegated to run the myriad of enterprises he had either begun and left, or fixed and left.

There was a certain status to having a direct line to legendary

E.P., and those that did skirted the perimeter of E.P. Taylor like dancers around a maypole. They spoke on his behalf, and ultimately created a buffer zone between Taylor and all the rest.

Taylor's Achilles's heel appears to be that he was not always a good judge of character. When it came to the people surrounding him, sometimes he got lucky, but often not, as evidenced by the fact that the great empire he built is no longer so great.

"Mr. Taylor was easily taken in," offers Beth Heriot, "easily conned. He took people at their word."

"In the sports pages he was called an entrepreneur; in the business pages—a tycoon," adds cousin Michael Magee. "But really, he was a great salesman—happiest when he was charming the birds out of the trees.

"And you know what great salesmen admire? A great sales pitch."

■ **5 OCTOBER 1956. BELMONT PARK, NEW YORK**

The six-furlong Anticipation Purse, a prep for the Belmont Futurity, was two weeks after the discovery of Nearctic's quarter crack. Nearctic's rider was U.S. jockey Nick Shuck; his trainer was Charley Shaw.

Nearctic blasted into the lead, only to find himself closely pursued by Bold Ruler, the highly motivated son of Nasrullah. Bold Ruler had won five of his six starts with top U.S. jockey Eddie Arcaro in the saddle. He was determined to be first to the wire.

At the half-mile Nearctic had the lead, but Bold Ruler was at his shoulder, tracking him stride for stride. After giving everything he had in the first half of the race, Nearctic finished an exhausted fifth, three lengths behind the winner, Bold Ruler.

"With that quarter crack chewing into him," said Bill Reeves, "it's a wonder the horse did what he did. After a half mile, it would start biting. The horse has got it in his head he's meant to be running, but his body is hurting."

■ **13 OCTOBER 1956. BELMONT PARK, NEW YORK**

The horse-racing fans flocking to Belmont Park that autumn afternoon were about to witness several great moments in North American racing. Many had come to Belmont Park to see the great Nashua run in what was to be his final race, the Jockey Club Gold Cup.

A son of Nasrullah, thus a grandson of Nearco, Nashua was a powerhouse. Foaled 14 April 1952, at Kentucky's Claiborne Farm, Nashua was born big and just kept getting bigger. He appeared ungainly as a yearling because he was growing so fast; but by the time he was two, Nashua was magnificent. He stood 16 hands high and appeared already mature. He was strong and he was handsome. His coat was a rich dark brown, adorned simply with a snip of white on his forehead and a band of white capping his right foreleg. And Nashua was reputed to have attitude: "Nashua, showing a trait that was to become associated with other offspring of his temperamental sire, seemed to have a mind of his own," wrote William Robertson in *The History of Thoroughbred Racing in America*

Nashua's jockey, Eddie Arcaro, put it more succinctly: "He can scare you!"

In the United States at the time, there were four separate groups conducting Thoroughbred championship polls: Triangle Publications, Inc., polled staff of the *Daily Racing Form* and *Morning Telegraph*; *Turf and Sport Digest*, solicited the views of selected sports writers and sportscasters; The Thoroughbred Racing Associations, Inc., asked racing secretaries at member tracks; and *Thoroughbred Record* magazine, used a mathematical scoring system, in which points were awarded for stakes victories.

In 1954, for the first time, all four groups were in accord: Nashua was U.S. Champion Two-Year-Old Colt. They also agreed that High Voltage, a grey daughter of the french stallion, Ambiorix, was the Champion Filly. (In later years the four groups were inclined to return to their habit of disagreement; although eventually everyone banded together to vote for—and dispute the outcome of—the Eclipse Award champions.)

As a three-year-old, Nashua stood 16.1 hands high, his girth measured 72 inches, and he was 1,200 pounds of sheer muscle. Now, at four and about to run the final race of his illustrious career, Nashua stood almost 17 hands high.

In the Carter Handicap at the end of June, Nashua had finished seventh, the only time he had been out of the money. He bounced back in the 1-1/4-mile Suburban Handicap on a fast track carrying

128 pounds to victory over Dedicate (111) with the fastest time of the year at Belmont Park for that distance. Then, in the Monmouth Handicap, on a muddy track and hauling 129 pounds Nashua scored his most decisive four-year-old conquest. Conceding 19 pounds to second-place horse, Mr. First, Nashua won by three-and-a-half lengths.

And then fell victim to colic.

The *Daily Racing Form*, posted a brief report on the state of Nashua's health almost every day of the more than two months Nashua spent recuperating. His first race after his illness was the weight-for-age Woodward Stakes, in which Mister Gus sailed by to beat him by two-and-a-half lengths.

Nashua's final race was the two-mile Jockey Club Gold Cup. He had won the race the previous year and his owners and fans were hoping Nashua could duplicate the feat and leave racing with a flourish. And he did. Nashua won in record time, by two-and-a-quarter lengths.

After the winner's circle festivities, Nashua's jockey, Eddie Arcaro, had to hustle to the walking ring and onto the back of his mount in the next race, the Belmont Futurity. The horse was Bold Ruler. Both Nashua and Bold Ruler were trained by (Sunny) Jim Fitzsimmons, and both were sons of Nasrullah.

Like Nashua, Bold Ruler's coat was a dark bay; he was adorned with a bit of white on his forehead and a bit of white capping his right hind leg. Slightly lighter in bone than Nashua, Bold Ruler was still a big, good-looking horse. At three, Bold Ruler stood 16.1-1/2 hands high and his girth was a hearty 74 inches. Bold Ruler had won his first five races, including the Youthful and Juvenile Stakes, twice defeating the highly-regarded King Hairan. In the second of these encounters, the Juvenile Stakes, Bold Ruler strained the muscles of his back and was in rehabilitation for more than three months. With Bold Ruler sidelined, King Hairan won five straight stakes races, including the Hopeful Stakes in which he defeated Nearctic.

When he returned to racing on 24 September 1956, Bold Ruler experienced his first defeat, to Nashville, also a son of Nasrullah. His next race was the Anticipation Purse, his prep for the Belmont Futurity, which he won after stalking Nearctic for the first half mile.

■ **13 OCTOBER 1956. BELMONT PARK, NEW YORK**

The next race on the card was the Belmont Futurity and Nearctic, trained these days by Charley Shaw, was entered in this top U.S. race for two-year-olds.

Why was Nearctic in the 1956 Belmont Futurity? He had a quarter crack and enervating pain. Yet, one week after finishing fifth to Bold Ruler, Nearctic was back in the starting gate. He was wearing blinkers for the first time. Nearctic tended to try to run out when in pain. Perhaps his handlers thought the blinkers would fool him into thinking he wasn't in pain.

Nearctic was once again pitted against Bold Ruler, and Eddie Arcaro, fresh from his Jockey Gold Cup win on Nashua. Nearctic's jockey was again Nick Shuk, who finished fourteenth in the Kentucky Derby earlier that year, on a horse called Besomer. (Shuk was never again asked to ride in the Kentucky Derby.)

Why would they pit this poor horse up against the best horses on the continent. And why didn't Windfields hire a top-flight jockey?

The rest of the field of thirteen juvenile horses was studded with powerful combinations; Nashville, considered Bold Ruler's chief rival, was ridden by Ismael Valenzuela; Nashville's stablemate, Cohoes, was teamed up with Ted Atkinson; and racing legend Bill Shoemaker was aboard Blue Spruce.

When the Belmont Park starter sounded the bell, Nearctic catapulted from the gate and flew into the lead, galloping for all he was worth. By the half he was out front by four lengths—over Bold Ruler, Cohoes and Greek Game, on the outside, and Nashville and Iron Liege on the inside. Nearctic set a brutal pace. As Nearctic began to tire, Eddie Arcaro sent Bold Ruler off in pursuit, and quickly opened up a three-length lead. After the race, Arcaro told the media that it was the easiest ride he had ever had on Bold Ruler. Nearctic finished eleventh.

"Nearctic stopped dead," recalled Bill Reeves. "It was impossible for the horse to go any further. That quarter crack must have been really biting. It seems to me that the horse was trying 110 per cent, but the people working with him—maybe 20 per cent."

■ 20 OCTOBER 1956. WOODBINE PARK, TORONTO

Nearctic was back in Canada, with Pete McCann. The first time Nearctic returned from the care of Charley Shaw he was crazed and sore. This time he was worse, but he was still racing, Avelino Gomez rode the colt in the mile-and-seventy-yards Coronation Futurity, a premier two-year-old event. Nearctic was part of a three-horse Windfields Farm entry. (The other two horses were Mrs. Taylor's Chopadette and her husband's Lyford Cay.) Of nine horses in the field, Nearctic finished fifth.

"Nearctic was the speed horse as usual, but if he can be judged on his race today, he lacks staying power or the will to stay," declared the *Daily Racing Form*. "Nearctic seemingly had no excuse after his display of speed. He stopped without apparent excuse."

Everyone seemed to have forgotten about Nearctic's quarter crack, which should have given Nearctic licence not only to pull up halfway through the race but refuse to leave the gate. McCann would have been concerned about Nearctic's quarter crack which is no doubt why, following the Coronation Futurity, he loaded Nearctic, Lyford Cay and Chopadette on to the horse trailer and shipped them to Windfields Farm. He said he was preparing them for the next big two-year-old race, the Cup and Saucer Stakes. To that end, he brought them back to Woodbine and worked the horses out of the starting gate, but then returned them to the farm.

The latest pervasive element to this story had begun; Thomas overruling McCann. Thomas reported directly to Taylor. McCann no longer did. Thomas had started choosing the races he thought suited the Windfields horses—whether or not their trainer agreed.

McCann became even more diffident. When it came to verbal combat, he knew he didn't stand a chance against Thomas, so he focused all his attentions toward what he knew was his strong suit, and continued to train, condition and settle Nearctic's fragile nerves. Which is why he took him away from Woodbine. The other two horses were simply along for the ride.

While this was going on, however, another event was taking place at the track that would affect both Nearctic and McCann; Horatio Luro, the suave and dapper Argentine horse trainer had come to Woodbine Park to run a four-year-old Chilean filly called Eugenia II in the Canadian International Championship Stakes.

For the first time, the Canadian International Championship had actually attracted international runners: the Australian horse, Prince Morvi; Wise Margin from New England; Eugenia II from South American. The race was to be contested over Woodbine's brand new turf course, considered to be the best in North America.

On the weekend preceding to the race, Luro arrived in Canada, to great fanfare with his horse, groom and stable jockey, Juan Sanchez. The big race was to be run on Saturday afternoon. On the Tuesday prior to the Canadian International, Luro ran Eugenia II in an allowance race. Ridden by Sanchez, she finished third in a lacklustre performance.

Several turf reporters questioned running Eugenia II so close to the big race. Others wondered if she would be scratched from the Canadian International Championship.

But some people caught on to Luro's ploy. One was Conn Smythe, owner of a string of fine Thoroughbreds, and the Toronto Maple Leafs, at the time, an exceptional hockey team. "As Luro inspected Eugenia II and was walking away, Smythe came by, winked broadly, and nodded in the direction of the filly," wrote Joe Hirsch in *The Grand Senor*. This chapter in Luro's biography was titled "Canadian Caper."

■ 27 OCTOBER 1956. WOODBINE PARK, TORONTO

The early pace in the Canadian International Championship was set by Canadian Champ, the horse that Bill Beasley had bought at Taylor's inaugural yearling sale. A son of the stallion Windfields, Canadian Champ had won the Queen's Plate and Canada's other two Triple Crown races. The Canadian Championship was his fifteenth three-year-old start: he had won 10 and was once second. On this day, however, Canadian Champ finished dead last. Eugenia II, ridden by Juan Sanchez, won the race by two and three-quarter lengths.

Conn Smythe was not among those surprised at the mare's sudden brilliance. He had placed a sizable bet on Eugenia II, watched the race with Luro, and left Woodbine that afternoon far wealthier than when he arrived.

Traditionally, following a major stakes race at Woodbine Park, the owners and trainer of the winning horse, along with friends and family, are invited to a champagne reception hosted by the Ontario Jockey Club. It was at this reception that Luro renewed his acquaintance with Taylor, who, as chairman of the Ontario Jockey Club, was official host.

The two men had met in California in the winter of 1948. Taylor was there to watch Windfields win the seven-furlong Arcadia Stakes. Luro had a horse called Endeavour II in the race and was among those invited by Taylor to join in a celebration of the victory. Taylor also took the opportunity to thank Luro for arranging to have the stallion Chop Chop sent to Canada.

It seems that one of Luro's clients, Mrs. Barclay Douglas of New York, wanted to find a home for Chop Chop, a son of Flares, who had won the 1938 Ascot Gold Cup for William Woodward Sr., chairman of The U.S. Jockey Club. Luro immediately thought of approaching Gil Darlington, whom he had met at Saratoga, and who was bloodstock adviser and, eventually, farm manager for Taylor. It was well known that Taylor was able to pay a good price for a horse.

Chop Chop was an excellent stallion prospect. Although his racing career had been cut short by an injury, in his 11 starts as a two- and three-year-old he was unplaced only once, prevailing over a number of good horses including Princequillo and Askmeknow. So in 1946 Gil Darlington leased the colt from Mrs. Barclay Douglas.

At some point Taylor purchased Chop Chop, who proved to be a successful sire. One of his first exceptional offspring was Canadiana, who won the 1953 Queen's Plate. He also sired Lyford Cay and Chopadette, but his most notable son was Victoria Park, a great racehorse, and a stellar sire.

Horatio Luro was charming, urbane and flamboyant. He dated chorus girls and movie stars, danced the tango and played polo. He drove flashy sports cars, was always beautifully dressed and occasionally broke. The Argentine was different from the other trainers in the United States —perhaps exotic especially to some of his female clients.

Horatio Luro was reputed to have a nervous disposition, and was frequently flying off to France or South America, leaving his stable in the hands of an assistant. Yet, Luro appeared to have nerves of steel when focused on one of his betting coups.

Was Horatio Luro a gifted trainer? A great horseman? I doubt it. But he was clever enough to have good horsemen working for him: Charlie Whittingham, Reggie Cornell, Thomas (Peaches) Fleming. For the most part, they tended to the horses; Luro tended to the clients.

Horatio Luro was born in 1901 in Argentina. His grandfather had emigrated to South America from the Basque Country on the French side of the Pyrenees in 1834. By the time his ship docked, the senior Luro had won enough money at cards to buy a cart, two oxen and a horse. Within ten years, he owned land covering hundreds of square miles. He raised cattle and began a meat packing operation.

As a young man, Horatio Luro, by his own account, was a playboy. At one point he followed a girlfriend onto a ship for France and ended up as a car salesman in Paris. After two years he returned to Argentina where he continued selling cars, expensive cars.

One day the very wealthy and socially prominent Mechita

Santamarina walked into his shop. She was going to Paris, and invited Luro to come along. She also apparently offered him a string of polo ponies. So off he went, back to Paris. In 1931 Horatio and Mechita were married. They lived in grand style, compliments of Mechita's family. Horatio Luro played polo for several years. According to *The Grand Senor*, "Mechita, who took an occasional drink, became jealous of every girl who looked at Horatio. Many did."

When they returned to Argentina, they lived in a palace belonging to Mechita's family. It is not clear what happened between Horatio and Mechita, but his biography notes that he "had been going with a lady from a prominent family in Chile while trying to obtain a divorce from Mechita..."

The woman went to Paris, so, of course, Luro followed, apparently keen to marry her, but she vanished back to the bosom of her family, who were not anxious to meet with the disapproval of the powerful Santamarina family.

On the way back to Argentina, Luro detoured to the United States and saw the possible market for South American horses. He returned to Argentina and, in 1937, brought the first of many consignments of South American horses to the United States.

Luro teamed up with a young jockeys' agent, Charlie Whittingham (who would become a U.S. Hall of Fame horse trainer). Whittingham had no horses of his own, and Luro had a couple of horses from Argentina, so their arrangement was simple: Whittingham trained the horses and Luro charmed owners.

Whittingham suggested that they go to Seattle, where they obtained a favour from his friend, the president of Longacres racetrack. Knowing that the pair didn't have much money, he had his racing secretary write a race to suit Dandy, one of their horses. Dandy won, providing them with enough cash to pay their bills and move on to the next race meet.

They were attracted by an advertisement for the Spokane Derby at Playfair Race Course in Spokane, Washington. The race offered a lucrative purse and because Dandy was not known to local horse racing fans, there was every likelihood they could organize things to their advantage. Not only was there a purse to be won, but there were bets to be cashed.

In Spokane they entertained lavishly in anticipation of a victory by Dandy to pay their expenses. Several days prior to the Spokane Derby, however, Dandy fell sick. His temperature was 104 degrees and he was coughing. A local veterinarian brought Dandy's temperature down, but could do nothing for the cough.

Whittingham confided their dilemma to the owner of the hotel, who was not amused. He pointed out that if Dandy was scratched they might find themselves in difficulty, because there were a number of shady characters who had a lot of money on this race.

Given this threat, they opted to run Dandy, somehow managing to keep the horse's illness a secret. Dandy went to the starting gate as the post-time favourite. Poor Dandy. He managed the first half-mile, but crossed the finish well after the others.

Apparently the hotel owner, apprized of Dandy's condition, wagered accordingly and won a bundle. Luro negotiated a 30-day note to cover the hotel bill, and he and Whittingham left town. Joe Hirsch summed up their adventures as "racing their stable up and down the West Coast, with a sense of timing that always kept them a step ahead of the sheriff."

During WW II Charlie Whittingham joined the U.S. Marines. Luro went to Miami. He had four unexceptional horses, no money and no partner.

According to *The Grand Senor*, "he was living on Miami Beach at the time in a small hotel. One evening, before going to dinner, he ransacked his quarters quietly and then departed. When he returned that evening, he began to shout: "Help! Police! I've been robbed!"

Luro benefitted heartily from this bit of chicanery. Not only did the hotel manageress agree to defer his hotel bill, but local newspapers ran stories of the unfortunate horse trainer from Argentina, and people sent him money.

Luro found a new assistant, Reggie Cornell, who would become famous as the trainer of the great Silky Sullivan, one of the most glamorous and exciting horses in U.S. turf history.

While working for Luro, Cornell travelled with the horses. Luro travelled by automobile. Cornell attended to the horses; Luro attended the parties. Among the horses that Cornell fed, conditioned and trained, was Princequillo, a horse Luro had claimed for $2,500 for his client, Princess Djordjadze who Luro had apparently met in Paris when she was married to a cousin of the Czar of Russia. Born Audrey Emery of Cincinnati, the princess had since married another Russian nobleman, Prince Dimitri, when Luro convinced her to make an investment in horses.

It is difficult to gage Princequillo's abilities as a racehorse, as he raced during the war years when U.S. racing was severely curtailed. Despite a number of physical problems, Princequillo won several noteworthy races, including the Jockey Club Gold Cup. It would be as a stallion, however, that Princequillo would achieve fame. And Luro, fortune.

During Princequillo's later racing days, in 1944 Luro was on the brink of a breakdown. His doctors apparently recommended that he take a sabbatical from his stressful career. He sold his share in Princequillo to the princess for $50,000, a great deal of money. Luro sailed to South America for a holiday just as U.S. racing was temporarily stopped.

When the war was over Luro returned to the United States. In the fall of 1946 he moved to California where he shared an apartment with Felix (Fe Fe) Ferry, a Roumanian who had produced shows with legions of chorus girls for the casino at Monte Carlo, and who, upon moving to Hollywood became a movie director.

Every weekend the two men entertained hordes of actors, actresses, stars and starlets at their Sunset Boulevard apartment.

Horatio Luro played polo with the rich and famous, and gave elegant performances of the tango at the celebrity dinner-dances. He imported South American horses to the United States, and continued to organize betting coups.

In *The Grand Senor*, author Joe Hirsch explains one such coup. It was, extremely well thought-out and in my opinion, outrageously bold.

Clear Sweep was owned by a friend of Luro's in partnership with two other Chicago gentlemen. They wanted to dissolve the partnership—after cashing a major bet.

They gave Luro six months with the horse, during which time he deduced that Clear Sweep was not much of a racehorse. Throughout the winter Luro entered Clear Sweep in races he was bound to lose. Anyone reading Clear Sweep's past performance charts would have thought that the poor horse didn't have a hope. Meanwhile, however, Luro and his stable rider, Jorge Contreras, were training the horse for a distance race.

The following spring, instead of shipping his horses to Keeneland for the race meet that precedes Derby week at Churchill Downs, he brought Clear Sweep directly to Churchill Downs just in time to be in the final race on Kentucky Derby Day. The year was 1952. Which was extremely fortunate for Luro. Surely anyone who knew Luro well would have figured out what he was up to when they realized that he was running a horse who would be going off at very long odds—and in the last race of the day.

But lady luck was with Luro this day. For this was the year that the formidable Native Dancer was beaten at the wire in the Derby by an obscure animal named Dark Star. Native Dancer had never been beaten, nor would he be beaten again. People were stunned.

Amid the post-Derby chaos and controversy, Luro prepared his coup:

"The horse had been stabled at Churchill Downs in the barn of the popular veterinarian, Dr. Alex Harthill, and Luro had made two requests of the Good Doctor that morning," wrote Hirsch. "The first was to be sure the groom at the barn put cold-water bandages around the front ankles of Clear Sweep before leading him over to the paddock. The other was for the prominent Dr. Harthill not to stand near Luro while Clear Sweep was being saddled."

At the time, Luro was a house guest of Warner Jones, chairman of the Board of Churchill Downs. On Derby Day Luro attended a luncheon hosted by the Hancocks of Claiborne Farm, and spent the afternoon in the VIP lounge with the celebrities and luminaries of Kentucky's Thoroughbred community.

For someone who apparently had suffered from a nervous condition, the man appeared to have nerves of steel. Prior to the final race Luro walked calmly to the paddock. En route he was approached by Toots Shor, a well-known New York restaurateur, who asked him about Clear Sweep. Horatio Luro replied: "He had not shown anything to warrant support." And kept walking.

Luro then calmly returned to the box of the chairman of Churchill Downs, to witness the final stages of this betting coup he had been working on for six months.

Clear Sweep won the race and paid $38.50 on a $2 win ticket.

■ **3 NOVEMBER 1956. WOODBINE PARK, TORONTO**

Avelino Gomez was teamed up with Nearctic for Canada's second major two-year-old event, the mile-and-one-sixteenth Cup and Saucer Stakes. There were ten horses in the field.

Nearctic drew post position seven. He was slow out of the gate, lying eighth at the start of the race. He managed to get up to third at the top of the stretch, but faded.

The race ended in a dead heat between Ali's Pride and Lad Ator. Third was Lyford Cay. Mrs. Taylor's Chopadette was fifth and Nearctic a tired, sore eighth.

After the Cup and Saucer Stakes, Nearctic was shipped to Windfields Farm, this time for a well-deserved rest.

Several weeks later, Taylor was in New York where he and Horatio Luro met once again, according to Luro, *quite by accident*. The accident occurred in the office of Dr. Cooper Person, husband of Liz Whitney, of one of Luro's clients.

Eventually the conversation came around to Nearctic.

Luro's account, as told to Joe Hirsch in *The Grand Senor* is that: "When Taylor saw how cleverly Luro had prepared Eugenia II to win the Canadian Championship at 13 furlongs, he felt he was the man to teach Nearctic how to carry his blazing speed a distance of ground."

I am not convinced that this was entirely the case. Luro was shrewd, urbane and charming—qualities Taylor admired. Taylor was an enthusiastic, wealthy, well-connected Thoroughbred owner—qualities Luro admired.

Nearctic was obviously a horse of great quality, beautifully bred, big, powerful and handsome. He could run a hole in the wind. No one really knew how to deal with him—no one except Pete McCann.

But, Pete was a man of very few words, and even when he did speak, he was generally overruled or disregarded by the more voluble Luro and Joe Thomas.

The fact that Nearctic was Canadian-bred did not help people's perceptions of him. At the time, Americans could not perceive that Canadians were capable of producing Thoroughbreds of quality. This perception hasn't changed in any meaningful way, but back then, Canadian horses and trainers were not taken very seriously. Neither Nearctic nor Pete McCann were accorded much respect.

In the late fall of 1956, Nearctic was once again taken from McCann and sent, this time, to Luro. During that fateful afternoon at the doctor's office in New York, Luro explained to Taylor that he trained his horses in California in the winter—and he would be happy to take Nearctic with him.

"At the time, we thought we had ourselves a Kentucky Derby colt in Nearctic," said Joe Thomas, "and we let Horatio take him. We certainly felt he was a Queen's Plate winner."

There are many flaws in this argument, not the least of which was that Luro had never entered a horse in the Kentucky Derby, much less had the credentials to condition a Derby horse. And if it was a Queen's Plate they were looking for—Pete McCann had already trained three Plate winners.

"Why would they not have sent Lyford Cay?" asked Bill Reeves. "He beat Nearctic in the Coronation and the Cup and Saucer. And he didn't have a quarter crack. That would have made more sense."

There appears, however, to be little logic in this part of the story.

When they got Nearctic to California, Luro faced a serious dilemma. He had convinced Taylor that he, Horatio Luro, could train Nearctic, prepare him for the Kentucky Derby. Should he succeed in getting Nearctic into the Kentucky Derby starting gate, Taylor would no doubt employ him to train other Windfields horses.

The one thing Luro seems to have overlooked in this plan was the horse. He had presumed that the sharp, fast workouts that Charley Shaw had been giving Nearctic were what had made him overeager and out of control when Luro saw the horse at Saratoga. Thus Luro reasoned, what Nearctic needed were long, slow gallops. The theory was sound, but Nearctic proved impossible to ride. No one Luro knew was up to the task.

And so there he was, trying to find someone who could actually ride the horse.

Perhaps Nearctic understood how obtuse humans were and that by becoming unridable, he could give himself a rest. The respite, however, was too brief to mend his quarter crack.

Luro's prayers for a rider were answered when champion European jockey William Raphael (Rae) Johnstone arrived in the backstretch of Santa Anita racecourse. The Australian had ridden some thirty classic victories over Irish, English and French courses. Johnstone was an accomplished jockey, particularly proficient at riding a waiting race. This talent gained him the nickname of Le Crocodile by French horse racing fans, who saw him surface late in a race and then devour the competition.

Johnstone's impressive European riding career got off to a slow and bumpy start. Johnstone had journeyed to England in 1933, confident that the British horse-racing world would applaud his arrival. Not only did they not roll out the red carpet, but the British Jockey Club stewards refused to grant him a licence to ride in England.

The stewards were not obligated to explain their decision; they simply said that they were not issuing any new licences at the time. Some people, including Johnstone, were convinced that their refusal was based in the rumour that back home in Australia, Johnstone had a reputation as a wild and unruly rider.

Johnstone had spent his savings getting to England, and he was stranded without an opportunity to work. Instead of despairing, however, Johnstone turned the situation to his advantage. He befriended jockey Steve Donoghue, considered by many to be the best British rider ever. Johnstone travelled from track to track in England with Donoghue, learning all he could of both Donoghue's considerable riding skills and the idiosyncracies of the British racecourses. Or at least so he thought.

Charming and hugely talented, Donoghue also had acrimonious relationships with owners and trainers. In attempting to ride on the best horse in any race, Donoghue frequently broke contracts, ignored retainers, and evaded commitments. Time and again he offended and enraged owners. Despite his brilliance, a number of British trainers refused to hire him. (It is said that when approached by King George V's racing manager, Donoghue replied: "I should like to ride for his Majesty, my Lord, but I'm afraid his horses aren't good enough.")

Still when Donoghue rode Manna to victory in the 1925 English Derby at Epsom, it marked his fourth Derby victory in five years. He had become a great favourite with British racing fans.

One of his celebrated mounts was the endearing and enduring campaigner, Brown Jack. Only one other horse, the extraordinary steeplechaser, Arkle, has ever been as popular as Brown Jack, and that was four decades later. Brown Jack was bred in Ireland in 1924 and brought to England as a steeplechase prospect. By the time he was four years old, Brown Jack had become a decent hurdler. Donoghue approached Brown Jack's trainer and told him that the horse was too good to be jumping — he should be racing on the flat. Donoghue also offered to ride him. So it was that Brown Jack and Donoghue won the Ascot Stakes.

Brown Jack continued racing on the flat until he was ten, winning 24 races including the long-distance Queen Alexandra Stakes at Ascot six years in succession. Donoghue was always aboard. The British adored Brown Jack and no doubt Donoghue's association with him enhanced the rider's popularity.

In 1933, when he met Johnstone, Steve Donoghue was a year

short of his 50th birthday. He would soon be retiring from race riding, but wanted to win one more English Derby, on a horse called Colombo.

Colombo was owned by Lord Glanely, a working-class Devon lad who, as a youngster, went to sea, found employment with a shipping company, battled his way to the top, and eventually started his own shipping company. In 1918 he was knighted for wartime services.

In 1919, his horse, Grand Parade, won the English Derby. During the next decade, Lord Glanely spent a fortune on Thoroughbred yearlings. Often the purchases were ill-advised, but Grand Parade cost only 470 guineas, and Colombo, the horse Donoghue had decided would be his latest Derby winner, cost Lord Glanely only 510 guineas.

Colombo apparently had a difficult temperament, and Captain Hogg, Lord Glanely's trainer, approached Donoghue to ride Colombo in one of his early gallops. The horse settled with Donoghue and worked wonderfully. The leading British jockey, Gordon Richards, rode Lord Glanely's horses, but twice during Colombo's two-year-old year Richards had commitments elsewhere, and Donoghue was hired as a substitute. He rode Colombo to victory in both races—the Richmond Stakes at Goodwood and the Imperial Produce Stakes at Kempton, Colombo's final race of the season. Colombo was unbeaten and at the top of the Free Handicap at the end of the year.

Donoghue was not only convinced that Colombo would win the English Derby, he was certain the horse would win the British Triple Crown. Donoghue was also confident that he would be hired to ride Colombo in the British classics.

"So certain was he of this that he did not indulge in any of his usual wheeling and dealing about the ride," according to *The Faber Book of the Turf*, "nor did he make any direct approach to Lord

Glanely, but in his happy-go-lucky way went off at the end of the season on a holiday to South America without leaving a forwarding address."

It seems that Donoghue's instincts were correct, but Lord Glanely was unable to locate him. So Lord Glanely began looking elsewhere and approached Rae Johnstone, who had wisely stayed behind in England, while Donoghue was off in South America. Johnstone accepted Lord Glanely's offer instantly.

When Donoghue returned from his vacation and discovered that Rae Johnstone would be riding Colombo, he was shocked and very, very upset. Despite Donoghue's protestations, Lord Glanely refused to take Johnstone off Colombo. Donoghue ended up accepting a ride on Mediaeval Knight in the 1934 English Derby. Mediaeval Knight had no real hope of winning, instead he was entered by trainer Fred Darling as a pacemaker for his other entry, Easton.

In less than a year Johnstone had gone from watching British horse races from the sidelines, to riding Colombo, the hugely popular British champion. Colombo won his first start of the season, the Craven Stakes and went on to win the classic Two Thousand Guineas.

In the parade ring prior to the Two Thousand Guineas, however, Colombo broke into a sweat. It was the first time since his early racing days that Colombo had showed signs of anxiety. By the start of the race Colombo appeared to settle down, and galloped off in his brisk stride. When Colombo faltered in the closing stages of the race, Johnstone drew his whip and Colombo prevailed, by a neck over Easton.

The English Derby is not an ordinary classic. According to Federico Tesio, it is considered the one horse race that defines the Thoroughbred:

"The Thoroughbred exists because its selection depended not on experts, technicians or zoologists, but on a piece of wood: the winning post of the Epsom Derby. If you base your criteria on anything else, you will get something else, not the Thoroughbred... the conditions of the Derby have remained unchanged and its validity unquestioned; it is the Epsom Derby which has made the Thoroughbred what it is today."

The historic Epsom course features one and one-half miles of twists, turns, hills and dales. It is the most gruelling and demanding classic course in the world, requiring speed, stamina, agility, ability and adaptability of the horses. It also requires a great deal from the jockeys. Talent, fitness and instant reflexes are essential. Experience in riding is also critical—but this would be Rae Johnstone's first English Derby.

On Derby day so many fans believed Colombo to be invincible that he was installed as the overwhelming favourite. Lord Glanely was so convinced of a victory that he commissioned his favourite restaurant to prepare a grand celebratory dinner for himself and his friends.

The second the tapes went up Donoghue rode his pacemaker, Mediaeval Knight, into the lead along the rail. Johnstone tucked Colombo right in behind Mediaeval Knight. Perhaps he thought his hero and mentor would guide him through all the stages of this great horse race. Easton and Windsor Lad were galloping slightly behind Colombo, toward the centre of the course.

At Tattenham Corner Mediaeval Knight began to run out of steam. Charlie Smirke seized the moment and sent Windsor Lad soaring past Mediaeval Knight. So did Gordon Richards on Easton. The two seasoned British jockeys knew that Donoghue's horse was merely a pacemaker and had positioned their horses off the rail in order to have clear running room. By the time Johnstone realized what had happened, he was hemmed in by a wall of horses. And there he sat, no doubt to the horror of Lord Glanely and everyone else with money on Colombo—which was the vast majority at Epsom and throughout England.

Eventually a small space opened and Johnstone sent Colombo off in pursuit. The courageous colt did his best, valiantly catching up to Easton. When the horses flashed past the famous finish post, Windsor Lad was the winner a length in front of Easton, who managed to hold off Colombo by a scant neck.

It is safe to say, that at that moment in time, Rae Johnstone was the most unpopular man in Great Britain. Some speculated that the British jockeys resented this "foreigner" getting the ride on the favourite and had ganged up to stop Johnstone. Other claimed he had been duped by Steve Donoghue.

Perhaps the reality is two-fold. Like almost everyone else, Johnstone believed Colombo to be invincible, but being inexperienced in Derby riding, he had miscalculated the dynamics and had stayed on the rail far too long. Simply put, Johnstone gave Colombo a bad ride.

Needless to say, before the sweat under Colombo's saddle cloth had dried, Rae Johnstone's contract to ride Lord Glanely's horses was rescinded. As no one else would hire him, he left England in considerable disgrace, and began riding in France.

While Rae Johnstone would never be forgiven for his ride on Colombo, he did, eventually vindicate himself, at least marginally, in the eyes of British Thoroughbred horse racing. From 1947 to 1956 he rode the winners of ten British classics, including three English Derbies: My Love, 1948; Galcador, 1950; and Lavandin, 1956. In none of these races did he hug the rail as he did with Colombo, instead he could be found steadfastly in the centre of the course.

Once he became successful on European race courses, Johnstone frequently spent his winters in California, and occasionally drove out to Santa Anita to exercise a horse or two to keep himself fit. Whenever he raced a horse in France, Luro claims to have always hired Rae Johnstone. So it was logical that, when Johnstone arrived at Santa Anita's backstretch in December 1956, he would seek out Horatio Luro.

Horatio Luro relied on his "assistants" to train the horses. His first assistant, Charlie Whittingham, became a highly respected trainer and U.S. Turf legend. Other assistants were responsible for the two most famous horses in Luro's shedrow—Princequillo and Northern Dancer. While Pete McCann worked with Northern Dancer as a yearling, when the horse was given over to Luro, it was his assistant, Peaches Fleming, who did the training.

But when Luro commandeered Nearctic from Pete McCann, there is no indication that Luro had an assistant, so he appears to have been on his own in this venture. It may well have been that Luro was in pursuit of Taylor as a client, without bargaining on this wild and crazy horse. One thing is for certain: Luro was far more successful at training Taylor than Nearctic, or any other Taylor horses for that matter.

When it came to the defining the term "horse trainer," Pete McCann and Horatio Luro were worlds apart. Pete McCann arrived at the track long before dawn to check on his horses, to supervise their individual needs, to ride them out around the sand ring or the training track. Pete would be just finishing up at about the time Luro would roll into the backstretch.

Luro had style and flair. He arrived in a flashy sports car. He arrived immaculately dressed—riding britches, highly polished riding boots, jacket and vest. He left immaculately dressed. Pete could be found holding a pitch fork. Luro simply held court.

When Nearctic arrived in California, Luro was neither able to handle the colt, nor did he have anyone working for him that could handle the colt, much less ride him. Luro must have been delighted at the sight of Rae Johnstone.

Luro apparently explained that he had a horse with a lot of quality, but that needed settling down. Curiously there was no mention of a quarter crack, just that Nearctic was a problem horse that ran all out. Johnstone accepted the challenge.

At 7:45 every morning Johnstone arrived at Santa Anita's backstretch, beautifully attired. At eight sharp, Johnstone was tossed up on to the back of Nearctic.

Horses are trained very differently on each side of the Atlantic. In North America they generally live at the track; and get their exercise galloping around an oval dirt track. In Newmarket, England, horses walk, trot, canter, and gallop over forty miles of lush turf gallops. So it seems conceivable that once Johnstone was introduced to Nearctic, he suggested to Luro that the horse would benefit from long, slow work. He must have recognized that the North American method of training— galloping around a dirt oval—would make Nearctic even more crazed.

Luro claimed he received permission from Santa Anita's director of racing for Johnstone to hack around on Nearctic in the secluded, wooded area of the track's downhill chute. Then Johnstone would ride him on a long rein and long stirrups in a controlled gallop on to the main track. Luo also claimed Nearctic gradually learned to settle down, but the idea of Nearctic casually hacking on a long rein like Pokey the Pony does not fit with his volatile nature. It is conceivable, however, that Johnstone did help Nearctic relax.

According to Luro, by the end of the winter, Nearctic was ready for action, but a quarter crack appeared. This is presumably the same quarter crack that had begun after the Carleton Stakes on 22 September 1956 and that had been documented in the *Daily Racing Form*.

If Nearctic was given any time to heal, it must have been brief, because he was shipped back East in the spring with the rest of the horses Luro had in his care. Luro leased a cottage at Belmont Park, where he set up shop for the racing season.

It is quite possible that neither Luro nor Thomas had the experience to recognize a quarter crack or to understand its implications. While a horse may show lameness before a quarter crack is apparent to the naked eye, once it begins to appear, the clinical signs are obvious. Cracks in the hoof may start at the coronary band at the top of the hoof and travel downward or, more frequently, begin at the weight-bearing surface and split upward.

While the hoof of a horse may appear to be a solid, rigid structure, it is actually elastic, expanding and contracting with each step taken. It is essential that the wall of the hoof, as well as the sole and frog—the underside—are able to bend and reform as the load moves on and off the hoof. If flexibility is lost, the wall tends to split. Left unchecked, the quarter crack will worsen.

■ 1 JULY 1957. BELMONT PARK, NEW YORK

Nearctic was entered in the six-furlong Manhasset Bay Classified Handicap, his first race of the season, and he was favoured to win. Horatio Luro was listed as Nearctic's trainer; his latest jockey was a diminutive Irishman by the name of Conn McCreary. He is the sixth jockey to ride Nearctic in a race.

Usually first out of the gate, Nearctic was beaten by Roommate, but Nearctic wasn't long in catching up. He took command of the field at the top of the stretch, but on the day he was no match for Dancing Fleet. As ever, his spirit was willing, but Nearctic had not raced in eight months, and it appears he didn't yet have his racing legs under him. And then there was the ever-present quarter crack.

Conn McCreary went to the whip on Nearctic, but the horse had no reserves, crossing the wire second by a distant six lengths.

It would be almost a month before they started Nearctic again.

■ 26 JULY 1957. BELMONT PARK, NEW YORK

Nearctic's next race was the six-furlong Westbury Purse allowance race. He was still living in Luro's shedrow at Belmont Park, and Luro decided to give him another jockey: Juan Sanchez, Luro's stable jockey, the man who rode Eugenia II to victory in the Canadian International Championship. Sanchez was Nearctic's seventh jockey.

Nearctic hardly seemed the great warrior that he once had been. Gone was his usual spring from the gate. Gone was his fighting spirit. Nearctic finished a weary fourth, almost ten lengths back of the winner, King Hairan. According to the report, jockey Ted Atkinson whipped King Hairan at least a dozen times in the home stretch and stopped only in the final 60 yards.

Nearctic's problems were beyond Luro's capacity, and once again, the colt is returned to Pete McCann. Everyone else seemed to have given up on Nearctic. At least for the moment.

Nearctic was finally back in the familiar hands of with his old friend, Pete McCann. And another familiar person, Avelino Gomez, was back in Nearctic's saddle for the colt's Canadian 1957 debut, the six-furlong Sheraton Purse.

The starting bell clanged, the gates flew open, and Nearctic ambled out of the gate. In a field of eight horses Nearctic was eighth. Surely Nearctic's racing days were over. In the past ten months—from 5 October 1956 when he finished 5th in the Anticipation Purse—Nearctic had been started six times and failed to win a race.

Avelino Gomez, however, had not given up on him. He steered Nearctic to the inside rail, where there was lots of running room. It was as if Nearctic's old will to win suddenly found him, as he galloped aimlessly around the Fort Erie oval. Nearctic changed gears and went from trailing the field to the front by the half. He won the race by two-and-three-quarter lengths.

■ 19 AUGUST 1957. FORT ERIE RACECOURSE

Pete McCann continued to work with Nearctic in his morning workouts, and Avelino Gomez continued to ride him in his afternoon races, this time the six-and-a-half-furlong Lennox Purse. Nearctic blasted out of the gate and into the lead, and there he stayed, winning easily by 3-1/4 lengths.

Nearctic and Avelino Gomez were paired for the fifth running of the Canadian International Handicap, a mile-and-a-sixteenth over Woodbine's Marshall turf course. There were eight other three-year-olds in the field, but Nearctic outclassed the lot of them.

At the sound of the bell, Nearctic immediately sprinted to the front, opened up a long lead in the backstretch, and won by six lengths.

The *Daily Racing Form* reported: "It was Nearctic from start to finish... he zoomed around the first turn into a daylight lead while racing under restraint... On the backstretch he was under full steam and opened up about twelve lengths before going into the last turn. From there he was never threatened."

The next part of this story defies all logic. Now that the horse had won three races with Pete McCann, Nearctic was loaded into a van and driven to New York—to Horatio Luro. That Luro has had no success with Nearctic appears to be irrelevant.

When Nearctic began racing, he won his first five starts easily, and often brilliantly. He was of course, in the care of Pete McCann. In August Nearctic was vanned to Saratoga. He had a new trainer, Charley Shaw. In the Flash Stakes Nearctic was given a questionable ride, over a very sloppy track. He was eighth and ended up with bucked shins. A week later Nearctic was sent to the post in the Saratoga Special. The track continued to be sloppy. Nearctic had bucked shins and a new jockey. This one, George Walker, beat Nearctic in the head with his whip, when Nearctic attempted to escape the pain. George Walker hit Nearctic in the eye. Nearctic won the Saratoga Special.

If Pete McCann had been Nearctic's trainer at the time, it is likely George Walker would have ended up in hospital for his treatment of Nearctic. It would not have been the first time McCann, a former champion flyweight boxer, used his fists when someone abused one of his horses.

George Walker apparently was not reprimanded, instead, two weeks after the Saratoga Special, he was hired to ride Nearctic in the Hopeful Stakes at the end of the Saratoga season. Nearctic had become mentally unhinged and had not been given time for his bucked shins to heal. Not even Walker's whip could incite Nearctic and the horse finished a weary fourth.

Nearctic was then vanned back to Toronto and Pete McCann,

where the horse was given the better part of a month off. Pete wove his magic, exercised him every morning. Gomez rode Nearctic in the races. Nearctic won the Carleton Stakes with authority. And then the quarter crack appeared.

Did they give Nearctic time out? No. They put him back on a horse van and shipped him to Belmont Park, back to Charley Shaw. And they expected Nearctic to race against the top horses in the United States, top horses ridden by top jockeys, in particularly tough races. They gave Nearctic a new rider, but not a top rider. Nearctic had a quarter crack. Instead of dealing with his injury, they put blinkers on him, making him even more crazed. Nearctic raced with all his heart and strength against the mighty Bold Ruler. Nearctic finished fourth after the first encounter, eleventh after the second encounter.

By that point, the quarter crack was, no doubt, really bothering Nearctic, but some of his handlers appeared oblivious. According to Thomas: "I thought a couple of New York races in which he went head-and-head with Bold Ruler for extended distances were tremendous efforts, especially now that we realize what kind of a horse Bold Ruler was."

While Thomas may not have known what kind of a horse Bold Ruler was, most everyone else did, at least in the U.S. horse-racing circles. Early in the year, Bold Ruler was considered the best two-year-old in the country. Bold Ruler won his first five two-year-old races, including the Youthful and Juvenile Stakes, and twice defeated the highly regarded King Hairan. In the Juvenile, Bold Ruler strained the muscles in his back and was sidelined for more than three months. Bold Ruler had only just come back to the races when Nearctic ran against him.

On the morning after the Belmont Futurity Nearctic was back in a horse van headed for Canada and Pete McCann. That evening the van rolled into the Woodbine backstretch. Pete was told to get Nearctic ready for the Coronation Futurity. He argued against it.

He lost. So did Nearctic. He and Gomez finished fifth. Next McCann was told to run Nearctic in the Cup and Saucer Stakes. This time Nearctic and Gomez were eighth.

When Nearctic was two years old he was entered in a total of thirteen races. By way of comparison, his grandson, Nijinsky, ran five times at two.

Since his win in the Carleton Stakes back on 22 September 1956, Nearctic lost each of the four times he had been sent to the post. Two of those races, the Coronation Futurity and Cup and Saucer were considered the top two-year-old races in Canada—thus a preview of which horses would be the leading contenders the following year. From this, and most perspectives, Nearctic could not be considered a contender.

Still, according to Thomas, "At the time we thought we had ourselves a Kentucky Derby colt in Nearctic and we let Horatio Luro take him to California for the winter. Certainly, we thought he was a Queen's Plate winner."

Nearctic was shipped to California. No one was capable of riding him until Rae Johnstone showed up and he allegedly hacked Nearctic about the countryside. When Johnstone returned to Europe, Nearctic's quarter crack mysteriously reappeared.

Luro finally got Nearctic to the races in July 1957. Nearctic was second in one race, fourth in the other. Thus, the horse was returned to Pete McCann. And with Pete, Nearctic won his next three races.

So here comes the incredulous part. They took the horse away from Pete. They loaded Nearctic into a horse van and drove him to Belmont Park. They gave him back to Luro.

Nearctic found himself in the shedrow of Horatio Luro, a different stall, different feed, different water, different handlers, different voices, different atmosphere. And, almost every time he was in the walking ring prior to a race, a different rider was tossed up on his saddle.

■ **2 SEPTEMBER 1957 BELMONT PARK. NEW YORK**

Nearctic was entered in the one-mile Atlantic Beach Purse carrying J. Ruane, a jockey whose racing career was undistinguished, unsuccessful and brief.

Nearctic bounded out of the gate second, and moved up to the front. He was running first by a length at the quarter, and was leading by two-and-a-half at the half; but Nearctic crossed the wire second, two lengths behind the winner, Promised Land.

"Nearctic took an early lead, bore out during the last three-eighths of a mile and lost all chance," reported The *Daily Racing Form.*

"Bearing out? Sounds like trouble to me," commented Bill Reeves.

If Nearctic was bearing out, there must be a reason. Was he still sore?

Nearctic had been sent to the post six times in two months. Finally, there was a space—of three weeks—between this race and the next.

■ **24 SEPTEMBER 1957 BELMONT PARK. NEW YORK**

On opening day of the fall meet at Belmont Park, Nearctic was entered in the six-furlong Mitchel Field Classified Handicap. His jockey was Eldon Nelson. The race was won by Cohoes. Nearctic was second. But it was a very close horse race.

The speedy Cohoes grabbed an early lead, but Nearctic ran up alongside and dogged his every step. Coming into the turn, Nearctic was leading by a head. Careening out of the turn and down the stretch, Cohoes inched his way until he held a head advantage over Nearctic. Down the stretch they flew, the two gallant horses matching each other stride for stride. At the wire it was Cohoes by half a length, in what was a very thrilling horse race.

"Seventy yards out," reported the *Daily Racing Form*, "Nearctic looked a probable winner but Atkinson went at Cohoes vigorously with hand and heel and hit the line a half-length to the good."

"Went at Cohoes vigorously," can be translated as severe whipping, especially when it referred to Ted Atkinson. A leading North American jockey during the 1940s and 1950s, Atkinson was the first rider to have his mounts win over a million dollars. Off the track, Ted Atkinson, a native of Toronto, appeared studious and gentlemanly, and was nicknamed The Professor. On the track, however, he was known as The Slasher, his trademark being an arm pointing straight at the sky, ready to descend with the whip.

■ 2 OCTOBER 1957. BELMONT PARK. NEW YORK

Nearctic was still in the stable of Horatio Luro, and entered in a six-furlong allowance race with Eldon Nelson along for the ride. Nearctic was carrying 124 pounds, the highest weight in what sounds like a cavalry charge around Belmont's oval course. He was third at the start, moved up to second, powering along at the heels of Egotistical. But at the wire it was Out To Win, who won by a nose over Discard, ridden by Bill Shoemaker. Egotistical was third by half a length, Nearctic fourth by three-quarters of a length.

Nearctic was entered in the seven-furlong Vosburgh Handicap. Once again Nearctic was up against the team of Bold Ruler and Eddie Arcaro. Luro hired Conn McCreary to ride—the jockey who rode Nearctic in his first race of 1957, the Manhasset Bay Classified handicap. Conn McCreary was not entirely successful riding Nearctic back then—nor now.

Bold Ruler benefited, of course, from being ridden by the same jockey, Eddie Arcaro, and one trainer, Sunny Jim Fitzsimmons.

Bold Ruler was out of the gate and down the track before the rest of the pack knew what had happened. Ignoring the mud that was being kicked up by Bold Ruler's heels, Nearctic set off in furious pursuit. Nearctic wrestled the lead away from Bold Ruler and through the mud the two young stallions set a blistering pace—a pace that Nearctic was unable to sustain. After three-eighths of a mile, Bold Ruler had taken back the lead and was home free.

Bold Ruler won the Vosburgh Handicap by an amazing nine lengths, demolished a track record that had stood for fifty-one years. And he did it carrying 130 pounds over a sloppy track.

Nearctic, exhausted, staggered home dead last. He was carrying only 109 pounds. Something was terribly wrong, so, they loaded him into an van and shipped him back to Pete McCann.

■ 19 OCTOBER 1957. WOODBINE PARK, TORONTO, CANADA

Pete was instructed to get Nearctic ready to run in the Bunty Lawless Stakes. Pete knew that the horse was a wreck and needed time out, but any protestations were in vain. Thomas had taken over all reporting to Taylor. And, Pete McCann was pushed further into the background.

In addition, Thomas retained Conn McCreary to ride Nearctic. Why Conn McCreary, a jockey who has had no success with Nearctic, was chosen over Avelino Gomez, who had a history of success with Nearctic is beyond all logic. It would appear, however, that within the context of this story, incompetence was rewarded.

Nearctic's inclination had always been to bolt out of the gate and get to the front of the pack, when he was fit and well and not running in pain, he simply went to the front and stayed there.

Nearctic was first out of the gate in the Bunty Lawless Stakes and stayed there, creating the early pace, but in the stretch he began to fade. He finished fourth, a short head behind Canadian Champ.

"Nearctic took over rounding the first turn," reported the *Daily Racing Form*. "Canadian Champ at his heels waged a duel down the backstretch. Canadian Champ going in front, Nearctic battling valiantly. They ran each other into the ground and both were spent seventy yards from the wire."

This time they did not wait for Pete to work his magic and restore Nearctic back to his former fighting self. Instead they loaded Nearctic into a trailer and drove south to New York's Jamaica racecourse: ten more hours in a horse van. Back to Luro.

■ 6 NOVEMBER 1957. JAMAICA RACECOURSE, NEW YORK

Nearctic was in the starting gate with seven other horses on this sunny but chilly autumn afternoon, for the five-and-a-half-furlong Rockville Centre Classified Handicap. Nearctic was back with Luro, and Eldon Nelson was riding the colt.

Nearctic was held in second place for most of the trip; but despite "brisk handling," i.e., excessive use of the whip, he was unable to overtake the winner, Saci, who was ridden by Eddie Arcaro. Nearctic staggered across the finish third, two-and-a-half lengths behind the winner.

■ 18 NOVEMBER, 1957. JAMAICA RACECOURSE, NEW YORK

Less than a fortnight later, Luro entered Nearctic the six-furlong East Marion Purse, with Eldon Nelson as his jockey. Nearctic was never really in this race—he kept trying to escape throughout the entire contest. He finished fifth, eight-and-a-half lengths behind the winner, Little Hermit.

"Nearctic bore out badly the entire turn and raced extremely wide into the stretch," reported the *Daily Racing Form*. "Bore out badly" indicates that there was something wrong— physically, mentally or likely both.

■ 25 NOVEMBER 1957. JAMAICA RACECOURSE, NEW YORK

A week after running wide and "bearing out"—no doubt due to some stress-related physical pain or ailment—Nearctic was back in the starting gate. Luro had entered him in another six-furlong race, the Middleville Purse Allowance.

When the bell rang and the gates opened, Nearctic leapt from the gate. He was second at the start and, astonishingly, led the entire way. Nearctic won and Little Hermit finished fifth, six lengths behind Nearctic.

This, was the only time Nearctic won a race for Luro—a curious outcome considering how badly the horse fared in his previous two races. And the degree of pain the horse was suffering. A $2 bet on Nearctic, however, would have paid a good premium.

After the Middleville race Nearctic disappeared from the pages of the *Daily Racing Form*, only to reappear the following spring. Since there was no indication that Nearctic was shipped back to California to hack around the countryside with Rae Johnstone, I assume that Nearctic spent that winter in Canada.

"I was working across the road with the broodmares that winter," recalled Bill Reeves, "but I am pretty certain that this was when Pete spent all that time working with Nearctic, trying to get that quarter crack mended. Nearctic's hoof needed time to heal and to grow."

■ **19 APRIL 1958. FORT ERIE RACECOURSE, ONTARIO**

Still in the care of Pete McCann, the grand dark horse was reported to be looking good. He had put on weight and filled out over the winter, his dark hide glistened, and he was fit. Nearctic was entered in the third running of the five-furlong Bold Venture Stakes. His new jockey was Benny Sorensen, a former circus rider.

Nearctic jumped out into second spot at the start, and then he took over. Sorensen kept him tucked along the rail in the early part of the race. Coming into the stretch Nearctic was "slightly roused" by Sorensen and he won handily.

"Nearctic's effort was a corker," gushed the *Daily Racing Form*.

■ **3 MAY 1958 FORT ERIE RACECOURSE**

Under the care of Pete, Nearctic appears to be blossoming. Pete was riding Nearctic every morning, and the horse was more settled mentally.

For the third running of the five-and-a-half-furlong Vigil Handicap, Sorensen was back in Nearctic's saddle. It was the final afternoon of the Fort Erie spring meeting and a good-sized crowd had ignored the gloomy weather. It had been raining steadily all morning and a dense fog blanketed the course.

None of this seemed to bother Nearctic. He led the whole distance. Leaving the backstretch, Nirdar took a run at Nearctic, but before they reached the home stretch Nearctic distanced himself from the rest of the pack and won the race by two-and-three-quarters.

"It was a decisive front-running triumph," reported the *Daily Racing Form*. "Carrying top weight of 125 pounds, Nearctic skipped the distance over the muddy racing strip 4/5 of a second off the track record."

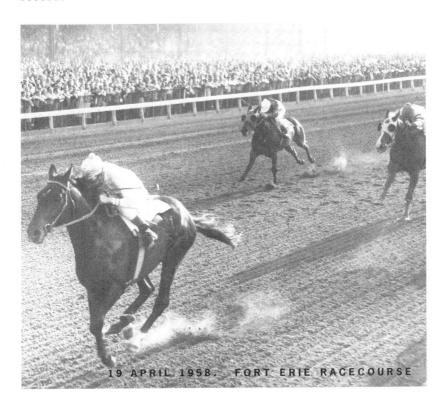

19 APRIL 1958. FORT ERIE RACECOURSE

19 MAY 1958.   OLD WOODBINE PARK, TORONTO

The beginning of Nearctic's four-year-old season seemed remarkably similar to the beginning of his juvenile year. He was physically fit, mentally sharp, and eager to run—and win. In the seven-furlong Swynford Stakes he continued to carry jockey, Benny Sorensen.

"A large crowd packed into historic Old Woodbine grounds to cheer Nearctic and cheer him they did," declared the *Daily Racing Form.*

Nearctic was a bit tardy coming out of the gate, but Sorensen hustled him along in order to get to the head of the pack. Thereafter, Nearctic put increasing distance between himself and the rest of the horses. Nearctic won by four-and-a-half lengths. Nirdar was second and Mr. Jive third.

■ 4 JUNE 1958. NEW WOODBINE PARK, TORONTO

Nearctic was entered in the six-furlong Jacques Cartier Stakes. Benny Sorensen continued to be his jockey. Nearctic took command early, established a long lead in the stretch and won with ease.

"Pete believed that his horses should be happy horses. And they should be fit horses," explained Bill Reeves. "That afternoon, Nearctic was a very happy, very fit horse."

Nearctic continued in the care of Pete McCann and was entered in the sixth running of the Canadian Maturity Stakes, a mile-and-sixteenth turf event for four-year-olds. Sorensen was in the saddle.

Nearctic established a huge lead of seven to ten lengths in the early stages. In the stretch, however, fatigue began to set in and Nearctic's stride was noticeably shortened. At that point, Our Sidar,

sensing that Nearctic was struggling, came charging up the stretch. The two horses crossed the wire in tandem. Nearctic triumphed, but just. He won by a nose.

"Nearctic won on heart that day," recalled Bill Reeves. "He didn't need to be that far out in front. It took too much out of him. He didn't have too much left in reserve."

Nearctic was entered in the sixth running of the Dominion Day Handicap, held on the country's birthday a national holiday now called Canada Day. The race is a mile-and-an-eighth for three-year-olds and up. The Ontario Jockey Club advertised "12 star-studded runners" in the field. The race had attracted two U.S. horses, Paper Tiger, owned by Mrs. E.D. Jacobs, and a horse called Spinney, which Luro had shipped in for the race. But the high weight of 125 pounds went to Canada's Mr. Jive.

As usual, Nearctic was the pacesetter; but the winner, after surviving a claim of foul, was Marshall Ney II. The eleven-year-old Irish-bred crossed the wire a scant neck ahead of Mr. Jive. A length back, was Winifred Taylor's Censor, and Nearctic, his head bobbing at about Censor's ears, finished fourth.

■ 5 JULY 1958. NEW WOODBINE PARK

Four days later, Nearctic was back in the starting gate for the Connaught Cup Handicap for three-year-olds and up, at a mile-and-a-sixteenth over the turf. Again Benny Sorensen was his jockey.

Carrying the top weight of 127 pounds, Nearctic galloped to the front of the eight-horse field soon after the start and there he stayed, setting the pace, for the first six furlongs. But then the fatigue set in, and Nearctic finished sixth. The winner, West Four, was carrying 115 pounds.

The Michigan Mile was considered by many to be Nearctic's finest hour (and was one of the few things people know about Nearctic). This race was the only time Pete McCann went to the United States as Nearctic's trainer. He brought Benny Sorensen along to ride Nearctic.

The day dawned sunny and cool, perfect weather for a horse race. Nearctic was up against some exceptional animals, and particularly the favourite, five-year-old Swoon's Son. Foaled on Friday the 13th, Swoon's Son was the leading money winner of the Thoroughbred crop of 1953, earning just under a million dollars for his owner, E. Gay Drake.

Swoon's Son raced for four years, and was a paragon of consistency. Unplaced only once in thirteen two-year-old starts— and that due to a disqualification—Swoon's Son won seven races, six in a row. At three, he won ten of his twelve races and was second in the other two. At four, he not only won six stakes while weighted down by at least 130 pounds, he also set a number of track records. At the conclusion of his five-year-old season, Swoon's Son was syndicated for a million dollars. He had gone to the starting gate fifty-one times, had thirty wins, ten seconds, and three thirds.

Swoon's Son was a exquisite-looking horse—a rich chocolate bay with a white diamond just beneath his forelock. A blaze started just below the diamond with a trickle that widened toward his muzzle.

The start of the Michigan Mile was delayed when jockey Conn McCreary tumbled off his mount, Red God, and fell backward out of the gate. When he stood up he was holding his wrist. (The previous year, in the paddock prior to this same race, McCreary had fallen off and hurt his shoulder.)

When the bell finally clanged and the gates sprang open, Nearctic bolted to the lead and there he stayed, which was fortunate. The starting gate was set only a short sprint from the first turn, where a traffic jam occurred. After the race, Dave Erb, who was aboard Swoon's Son, explained that his horse stumbled into Red God, who then had to pull up abruptly.

Nearctic, oblivious to the chaos behind him, continued to bound along at the front of the pack and out of harm's way. He cruised around the first two turns with speed and grace. Then Shoerullah slipped along the rail, out of the melee and set off in pursuit of Nearctic. But on this sunny afternoon, Nearctic was not to be caught. Nearctic carried Benny Sorensen across the finish two-and-three-quarter lengths ahead of Shoerullah and his rider, T.A. Gibbons. Swoon's Son finished eighth.

Incidentally, a two-dollar win ticket on Nearctic paid $44.40.

"When Nearctic arrived in Detroit, they said, 'Don't worry about him. He'll not threaten.' But when the man said 'go!' he was gone. He really took them by surprise," laughed Bill Reeves. "Nearctic ran the second quarter mile faster than the first. He seemed to love going around corners. He'd drop himself into it and ramble around."

A couple hours later, after Nearctic had been given time to cool down, Pete loaded him in the horse van and headed back to Fort Erie, where the rest of his racehorses were stabled. However, the Detroit racecourse was offering a bonus if a horse could win the Michigan Mile and the Detroit Sweepstakes, so Pete was told to bring Nearctic back to Detroit. Pete knew it was futile; he was, after-all, a former jockey. The competition hadn't taken Nearctic seriously in the Mile, underestimating the Canadian horse, his unassuming trainer, and his former circus-riding jockey. They'd be ready for them this time. Pete knew they wouldn't let him win a second time.

Nearctic was among the nine horses ushered into the starting gate for the Detroit Sweepstakes. Sorensen was in the saddle. Nearctic finished seventh, well behind Swoon's Son, who narrowly beat Mr. Jive. Shoerullah was last.

True to form, once Nearctic seemed to be doing well, Luro was on the phone to Thomas, and before long the horse was spirited away from McCann. Luro was at Saratoga and so Nearctic was vanned across the eastern states for the 32nd running of the seven-furlong American Legion Handicap. Sorensen was sent to ride the horse.

Coming into the stretch, Nearctic was sitting second behind Reneged, ridden by Bobby Ussery. Reneged drew away in the stretch and won by five. Nearctic "drifted out while tiring," reported the *Daily Racing Form*. He finished a dismal fifth.

From his performance, it appeared that Nearctic was suffering some physical ailment. It also sounds as if Nearctic was extremely weary. Whatever was wrong, it must be quite obvious, because Nearctic was vanned back to Canada and the care of Pete McCann.

It was almost a month before Nearctic was asked to race again.

1 SEPTEMBER 1958. OLD WOODBINE PARK, TORONTO

■ **1 SEPTEMBER 1958. OLD WOODBINE PARK, TORONTO**

Nearctic was entered in the seven-furlong Sandown Stakes. Sorensen steered Nearctic to the front along the rail on the first turn, where they saved ground. Dismissing several bold challenges from Nirdar, Nearctic galloped home two-and-three-quarter lengths in the clear, over second-placed Ali's Pride. Nirdar was third.

13 SEPTEMBER 1958. OLD WOODBINE PARK, TORONTO

Nearctic was entered in the Greenwood Handicap. Pete McCann was still Nearctic's trainer and exercise rider; his race rider was Sorensen.

In true Nearctic style, he immediately took his place at the front of the pack and quickly established a great distance between himself and the rest. Carrying a hulking 130 pounds, he won with speed to spare and was an easy four-and-a-half lengths over second-placed Pot Hunter.

Nearctic was entered in the mile-and-a-quarter Autumn Handicap. Sorensen was his jockey; Pete his trainer and exercise rider.

This is also the day of Pete's middle daughter's wedding. According to Reta McCann Irwin, her father did not escort her down the aisle, instead he chose to be with Nearctic in the walking ring at Old Woodbine Park.

"He did come to the reception," laughed Reta, "and as soon as he walked in the door someone yelled, 'Hey Pete, how did Nearctic do?'"

Nearctic, hauling top weight of 126 pounds, instantly assumed his long early lead and there he cruised until well down the stretch. But he started to tire and, in the last strides of the race, he was overtaken by the filly, Kitty Girl, carrying 117 pounds. Nearctic was second by three-quarters of a length.

4 OCTOBER 1958. OLD WOODBINE PARK

■ **4 OCTOBER 1958. OLD WOODBINE PARK**

Nearctic's next race was the six-furlong Seaway Handicap. He was carrying the high weight of 130 pounds, which included Benny Sorensen.

Jumping out of post position five, Nearctic went to the front on the outside. He quickly drew out into a long lead, entered the home stretch, and won the race with authority—three lengths over second-placed, Master Bart, carrying a mere 113 pounds. Nearctic also established a track record for six furlongs.

"Nearctic was nothing short of sensational when he lowered his own Canadian six furlong record and track record at Woodbine," declared the *Daily Racing Form*.

■ **13 OCTOBER 1958. OLD WOODBINE PARK**

For the mile-and-an-eighth Kingarvie Stakes, Nearctic was carrying 126 pounds. Benny Sorensen was in the saddle.

The heavy weights were taking a toll; his challengers were carrying considerably less—Our Sidar's burden was only 116 pounds. Ten pounds does not seem like a huge amount, but it was ten pounds of dead weight that, at the time, were lead bars inserted into pockets in the saddle cloth and thus were almost on top of the animal's kidneys.

Defeating the mighty Nearctic had become the focus of any number of Canadian Thoroughbred owners. Or did they simply wish to defeat Nearctic's owner?

Nearctic was predictable. As long as he was fit and sound, he ran to form—taking the lead, and staying there. So one strategy was to send out a "rabbit," a horse that would run like a cheetah for the first half, and force Nearctic to use up his energy in the duel. The rabbit would have no hope of winning, but with luck, a horse that had not used up its reserves could catch Nearctic at the wire.

The rabbit in this race was Top Turn, who set a sizzling early pace. And it took Nearctic a half mile before he had raced Top Turn to defeat. The rabbit ran out of gas, but as Nearctic pulled ahead by three lengths, he too was tiring. Sorensen had gone to the whip, but the colt did not have enough left to repel the challenge of Our Sidar. Nearctic finished second.

■ 18 OCTOBER 1958. OLD WOODBINE PARK

Nearctic's final Canadian race of the year was the Challenge Handicap, at six-and-a-half furlongs. Sorensen was in the irons and Nearctic was carrying 130 pounds once again.

Starting from post position five, Nearctic jumped into the lead, closely hounded by Arcandy. Nearctic finished second, a length behind Arcandy.

"It was a see-saw duel through most of the six-and-a-half furlongs," reported the *Daily Racing Form*. "The pair took turns taking the lead. Johnny Heckmann, who came from Chicago to ride Arcandy, had plenty of horse under him as they went to the wire, a substantial length ahead of Nearctic and Sorensen."

Nearctic had been sent to the post sixteen times that year. Nonetheless, Nearctic was loaded on to a horse van and driven not to the farm for some well-deserved rest, but back to the United States to Horatio Luro.

■ **NOVEMBER 1958. JAMAICA RACECOURSE, NEW YORK**

For the Sports Page Handicap, at six-furlongs, there were fourteen horses in the race. Conn McCreary had been hired to ride Nearctic.

"Luro didn't want to use Bennie," explained Bill Reeves. "I don't know why.

Nearctic staggered out of the starting gate thirteenth of fourteen horses; he finished twelfth.

There was something obviously wrong with Nearctic. He is no doubt exhausted, and probably lame. But did they send him to the farm to recover? No. Instead they fired the jockey.

■ **17 NOVEMBER, 1958. JAMAICA RACECOURSE**

Luro and Thomas entered Nearctic in the six-furlong Jefferson Handicap and replaced McCreary with Bennie Sorensen.

There were six horses in the field. Nearctic stumbled out of the gate and trailed the pack for most of the way. In the stretch Sorensen went to the whip and the weary colt finished third.

They sent Nearctic back to Pete McCann.

Nearctic was started three times in his five-year-old year. In these, Nearctic's final racing days, Pete McCann was Nearctic's trainer and exercise rider, and Bennie Sorensen was his race-rider.

■ **27 APRIL 1959. FORT ERIE, ONTARIO**

The first race that year was five-and-a-half-furlongs at Fort Erie. At the half Nearctic was in the lead, but only just. He was overtaken in the stretch, but he battled back. The best he could manage, however, was third, by a nose, behind Unity Courier and White Apache.

2 MAY 1959, FORT ERIE

Five days later Nearctic was entered in the Vigil Handicap, at five-and-a-half-furlongs. "Nearctic had speed from the start," reported the *Daily Racing Form.* "[He] opened a long lead on the turn and was not seriously threatened."

Nearctic won the Vigil, for the second consecutive year, this time by two-and-a-half lengths. He was made to carry 126 pounds, by far the most weight in the race. Unity Courier was given the next highest weight at 117 pounds. Our Sidar was given 113 pounds. The rest carried as little as 103 pounds.

Nearctic ran the six furlongs in 1:10-3/5, equalling the track record.

Following the Vigil Handicap, Nearctic was shipped to Woodbine racetrack. A week later he was entered in the seven-furlong Ultimus Handicap. By the half, Nearctic had battled his way to second place, but his limbs could no longer carry his fighting spirit. Even though Sorensen had gone to the whip, Nearctic caved in and crossed the finish line sixth in a field of seven horses.

"Windfields Farm's 1-4 favourite, Nearctic shocked the attendance of 20,722 in failure," reported the *Daily Racing Form.* The "unbeatable, Canuck," with top weight of 128 could not keep pace with his rivals. His performance was in keeping with the first "shocker" at Fort Erie when he was beaten in his 1959 debut.

"No excuse would be found for Nearctic unless it was weight—or perhaps he isn't as good as he was a year ago," the report mused. "He was gunning for the lead at the first turn and couldn't make it. He joined the pacemakers on the last turn and for a moment it appeared that he would take the lead. He weakened badly and faded out of the picture."

Later it was discovered that: "the handsome 5-year-old son of Nearco and Lady Angela may have had an excuse for his shocking defeat in the Ultimus Handicap... it was discovered that Nearctic was suffering from a blind splint. When it popped we don't know. And whether it hurt him on the weekend only Nearctic knows."

A splint is a bony enlargement that arises between the canon (metacarpal) bones of the forelegs, or (metatarsal) hind legs. The bumps can be as small as a tiny pea to the size of an egg; and are the result of ossification of ligaments on the metacarpal or metatarsal bones. The most common site is on the inside of the front fore. The usual causes are concussion or excessive training of young horses, and are most frequently encountered in horses under five years of age, prior to physical maturity. The amount of pain caused by a splint can vary.

Following the Ultimus Handicap, Pete McCann walked Nearctic back to the stables, knowing it was time to retire the volatile colt before he suffered a serious injury. And so, he sent Nearctic to Taylor's National Stud Farm with the intention of giving him the rest of the year off and beginning his stallion career in 1960.

Pete's plan for Nearctic was, however, premature. Windfields racing manager, however, had another agenda—Nearctic was to continue racing.

In the 13 May 1959, *Daily Racing Form,* columnist Frank Armstrong wrote, "Joe Thomas was inclined to think that Nearctic is becoming "cute," [meaning] he runs when he feels like it and perhaps [is] becoming undependable in his advancing years."

According to Armstrong, the splint on Nearctic's right foreleg was "of such a mild nature that it may not be necessary to apply the firing irons to correct the ailment. However should it be advisable to fire, and that decision will be made within hours, the horse will be out of training only about 10 days and will be able to keep his engagement in the Jacques Cartier Handicap, opening day headliner of Woodbine's summer meeting."

And indeed on 22 May 1959, the *Daily Racing Form* headline read: "Nearctic Blazes Speedy Five Furlongs: Windfields Star fully recovered. Clocked in 1:00-1/5 for Prep Over Good Woodbine Strip."

Several days later, Armstrong reported, "Joe Thomas was telling us that the suspected splint required no treatment and maybe the splint doesn't exist," and then added, "Joe expressed doubts that Nearctic would be as consistent in the sprints as he was formerly."

The report quoted Thomas as saying that Nearctic "has developed a sort of Dr. Jekyll and Mr. Hyde personality. Around the barn he is gentle and easy to handle... [but] this year he became a little rough when sent to the races. He has always been anxious to be off and running... Now he seems to resent competition when he doesn't have his own way, so he doesn't try."

"I just think that Nearctic had had it," suggested Bill Reeves. "I don't think it was the splint. He had certainly run under greater pain. No, Nearctic had had enough. He'd put in a lot of good years, a lot of hard work. He was ready to retire."

I suggested to Reeves that Pete McCann might also have had it, that he might have become weary of being expected to work his magic on Nearctic, only to have the horse taken from him over and over. Pete hated to see any animal hurt. Was it possible, that Pete simply pulled out of the game?

"Ah," replied Bill Reeves. "An interesting thought..."

The *Daily Racing Form* headline for Tuesday, 2 June, 1959 read: "Nearctic Is Retired From Competition: Windfields Horse To Serve at Stud."

The previous day, Nearctic was supposed to be running in the Jacques Cartier Stakes at Woodbine; but he wasn't entered in the race, nor was there any mention of his absence.

According to Federico Tesio, "Stallions who have raced until the age of six and have undergone stiff training seldom produce good offspring when they first embark on their new career. They have used up too much of their vitality in racing, and need time to rest and restore it." There can be little doubt that Nearctic had endured much. That he spent the rest of the year roaming his paddock and being tended to by Windfields stallion manager, Harry Green, would have done much to restore Nearctic's energy.

The following spring, Nearctic began life as a stallion with vigor and enthusiasm. Gil Darlington set Nearctic's stud fee low at $2,500. Still local Thoroughbred breeders chose to wait and see if Nearctic's offspring would amount to anything before sending their mares to this elegantly-bred horse.

In the spring of 1963, the first crop of Nearctic's progeny was ready to race. It was a small group, only fourteen; but they all started, and all were winners—a portent of things to come. The first winner was a chestnut filly named Holy Cow. Other members of this dynamic group were stakes winners Arctic Hills, Belarctic, Langcrest, Pierlou and, Nearctic's most famous son, Northern Dancer.

The odds that a Nearctic offspring would not only race, but win, were exceptional. Quite a contrast to Nearctic's generation of this potent genetic blend, and thus giving further credence to John Aiscan's research into the Nearco/Hyperion cross. From the perspective of the second generation his contention that: "Horses by sons or grandsons of Nearco, out of mares by sons or grandsons of Hyperion have less character and temperament problems," seemed prescient.

Nearctic sired fourteen crops, totaling 345: 173 colts and 172 fillies. An astounding 92 per cent of the colts started in races; 87 per cent were winners. And 80 per cent of the fillies started in races; 58 per cent were winners.

In the fall of 1964, Nearctic was joined by his son, Northern Dancer, in the stallion barn at the National Stud Farm. The previous year, Taylor had begun building a farm in Cecil County, Maryland, across the road from Mrs. Richard C. du Pont's Woodstock Farm. Taylor's farm was intended as a training centre. The location was ideal: there were a number of racetracks within easy vanning distance; and the rolling hills and luxuriant green meadows were perfect pasture land. Furthermore, the Maryland government smiled kindly upon the business of raising and racing Thoroughbred horses.

Three years later, Nearctic was sold for $1,050,000 to a Maryland syndicate organized by Taylor and Mrs. du Pont; Taylor kept ten of the 32 shares. Shortly thereafter, Nearctic was shipped to stand at stud at Mrs. du Pont's farm. Gil Darlington explained the rationale behind the move to journalist Jim Proudfoot, in the January 1967 *Canadian Horse:* "We're certain Northern Dancer is going to be a great sire, too," explained Darlington. "Now if you have a father and son standing at the same stud, you soon become overloaded with that blood."

But less than two years later, on 16 October 1968, Taylor announced that Northern Dancer was leaving Canada to stand at his Maryland farm, across the road from Nearctic.

Every day for the more than eight years between his retirement from racing and being loaded on the van and shipped to Maryland, Nearctic was cared for by Harry Green. Harry fed Nearctic, and groomed him, turned him out in his paddock in the morning, brought him back into the barn in the afternoon, and accompanied him each time he went to the breeding arena.

When Harry retired in 1973, he and his wife, Florence, drove to Maryland to visit Nearctic. It had been six years since Harry had seen his old friend. As he and Florence approached the barn, one of Mrs. du Pont's staff rushed across the yard and politely suggested that the strangers return during visiting hours.

Harry explained they had driven a long way to see Nearctic— he was too modest to mention he had looked after Nearctic in Canada. Suddenly there was a loud nickering from the barn. After six years, Nearctic still recognized Harry's voice, and the groom relented. As Harry entered the barn, an obviously ailing Nearctic struggled to his feet, bellowing and snorting. Harry finally confessed that he had once cared for Nearctic and asked if he might go into the stall. Reluctantly the groom assented, adding, "At your own risk, sir."

"Hello, Nicky, it's good to see you," said Harry, opening the stall door and walking slowly toward the stallion. Nostrils flaring with excitement, eyes bright, Nearctic hobbled over to Harry and butted him with his snout. Harry responded by stroking him on the neck. Soon Nearctic was nuzzling at Harry's pockets to see if his old friend had brought him any treats. (He had.) It wasn't long before Nearctic allowed Harry to wrap his arms around his neck. Tears streamed down Harry's checks. He truly loved this horse, and, in his way, Nearctic loved Harry.

A month or so later, I had the opportunity to spent time with Nearctic. I was writing *E.P. Taylor: The Horseman and His Horses* and had come to explore their Maryland farm. And, of course, to see Northern Dancer.

Mr. Taylor insisted that we also drive over to Mrs. du Pont's farm to visit Nearctic; Mrs. Taylor politely declined the invitation. It wasn't until we were in one of the farm station wagons flying across deeply rutted paths, that I began to understand Mrs. Taylor's reluctance. Taylor was a dreadful driver. The crux of the problem was that he seemed to be paying very little attention to the fact that he was behind the wheel of an automobile.

En route to Mrs. du Pont's farm, Mr. Taylor had decided to take me on a tour of Windfields Maryland Farm and elaborate on his plans for expanding this already extensive facility. He seemed to have thought it necessary to take the back roads. The sole redeeming aspect to this unconventional route to visit Nearctic was that we passed Mrs. du Pont's daughter Lana, out riding Kelso, one of the great U.S. horse racing legends. Kelso was a gelding and so when he was retired from racing, Lana hacked him around the countryside.

When we bumped past Lana du Pont, it seemed clear that we were now on the riding trails. However, Mr. Taylor was so absorbed in his plans for the future that he seemed not to notice. By the time we pulled up in front of Mrs. du Pont's barns, I was quite unnerved.

Nearctic was lying down in his stall, and did not get up for us. Mr. Taylor explained that Nearctic suffered from chronic lymphangitis in his left hind. Nearctic looked tired and old; but he was only nineteen. Between Harry's visit and ours, Nearctic's health had rapidly deteriorated.

Six weeks later, on 27 July 1973, Nearctic was euthanized.

EPILOGUE

Unravelling the mystery of Nearctic seems to have run full circle. It began when writing about Nearctic's grandson Nijinsky and concluded very close to that starting point. And, in the end, posed the question: Is it possible that Nijinsky, in some way, fulfilled the potential of Nearctic? For Nearctic was surely squandered.

Conversely, Nijinsky was given every opportunity to excel. When George Scott purchased Nijinsky at the 1968 Canadian yearling sale on behalf of Charles Engelhard, the colt was flown to Ireland, where he took up residence at Vincent O'Brien's Ballydoyle training centre in County Tipperary.

Ambling across 600 acres of serene countryside, Ballydoyle was considered one of the finest training facilities in the world. O'Brien's horses were treated like royalty. He spared no expense in creating an a five-star environment for the animals in his care. Nijinsky and the others lived in luxurious horse boxes—complete with padded walls and Dutch doors, open at the top so they could always look out. They trained over lush, gently rolling gallops. They were cared for by a large staff of carefully chosen professionals.

Still, Nijinsky did not instantly settle into his new lodgings. It appeared that he not only inherited his grandsire's regal stature and will to win, he was imbued with Nearctic's extreme nervous energy. As such Nijinsky presented O'Brien and his crew with countless difficulties. First, Nijinsky refused to eat O'Brien's finest Irish oats. Then he refused to come out of his stall—rearing and fighting those who dared coax him. Once that was resolved, he continued to be headstrong and explosive. On the gallops Nijinsky didn't like to work alongside the other horses. Eventually he settled down, but if the group stopped, even briefly, he would rear. O'Brien heaped no end of praise on his resident riders in their handling of Nijinsky: "They had the strength to handle him and the patience not to knock him about."

It wasn't just that Nijinsky won the British Triple Crown in 1970 — it was how he won that will remain forever in the memory of everyone fortunate enough to have witnessed his magic and his vast superiority over the other horses.

The major difference between how Nijinsky and Nearctic were handled is that O'Brien and his crew continually adjusted to the needs of Nijinsky. And I am reminded of something Dick Francis wrote in one of his novels: "As we serve them [the horses], they serve us." Those who served Nijinsky and helped him deal with his demons, and kept him fit and healthy, were surely rewarded as they watched this amazing horse fly past the winning post time and again. Indeed, we all benefitted from their devotion.

Nearctic on the other hand was forced to serve his masters. Where Nijinsky was treated like a prince, his aristocratic grandsire was frequently handled as if he were no more than an indentured servant to those whose motives were clearly not in the best interests of the horse. Instead Nearctic became a pawn in a bizarre power struggle.

Yet, in the end Nearctic prevailed. He had two things in his favour— impeccable bloodlines and Pete McCann. So as those of us who hold memories of Nijinsky in our hearts are grateful to O'Brien and his crew, we also owe a great debt to Pete McCann.

For without Nearctic we would have missed some of the greatest moments in Thoroughbred racing: Northern Dancer's heart-stopping, record setting 1964 Kentucky Derby; Dancing Brave's spectacular 1986 Prix de l'Arc de Triomphe; Peintre Celebre's breathtaking victory in the same race eleven years later; Arazi's magnificent

1991 Breeders Cup Juvenile; and Point Given's powerful 2001 Belmont; and Fusaichi Pegasus and Cigar and Favorite Trick and Charismatic and Dance Smartly and Swain and Singspiel and on and on and on.

PART FIVE
THE NEARCTIC LEGACY

In the summer of 1958 E.P. Taylor purchased the filly Natalma at the Saratoga yearling sale for $35,000. Her coat was a rich bay, her eye kind and intelligent with just a hint of wariness. There was a prominent vee-shaped white star beneath her black forelock. Her white marking tapered and continued down between her nostrils.

She was a blue blood: her sire and her maternal grandsire were two of the most famous grey horses in Thoroughbred sport.

Her sire was the great U.S. legend, Native Dancer. Her dam, Almahmoud, was a daughter of English Derby winner, Mahmoud. (To name this filly, Winifred Taylor joined the first three letters of her sire's name to the first four letters of her dam's name.)

Natalma spent the fall and winter of her yearling year at Windfields Farm in Oshawa. In the spring it was announced that Natalma would race in the United States, rather than Canada. In retrospect, it seems a curious decision. No other Windfields Farm horses started their racing life on U.S. racetracks. After all, Taylor was the great promoter of Canadian horse racing. He had built the new Woodbine racecourse, and it was in his best interest that the track flourish. It was therefore important for him to support this own venture. And although he and Mrs. Taylor kept residences in England and the Bahamas, and apartments in Montreal and New York, their home, and that of their three children, was Toronto. It was also the location of Taylor's main business offices. If he wanted to watch his horses run, Toronto was the obvious place to start them. Later, if they showed great promise, the horses then went to the United States to test their mettle.

Natalma was sent to the public stable of Horatio Luro. Natalma started twice at Belmont Park in the spring of 1959 and won both races. Her next race was the Spinaway Stakes in August at Saratoga. Again she won, this time by three-quarters of a length. She was, however, disqualified. It seems that her jockey, Bobby Ussery, had hit Natalma with his whip. In an effort to avoid the punishment, Natalma had ducked to the inside and bumped the filly Warlike, causing her to hit the inside rail. (Natalma's sire, Native Dancer, had also had great disdain for the whip.) Following the Spinaway, Natalma refused to go anywhere near the track.

After about a month of delicate handling, including ponying Natalma around the backstretch, Luro's staff were able to get the filly back in training. (Luro had left for France right after the Spinaway.) But not long afterwards, Natalma pulled up lame. The diagnosis: a small bone chip in her right knee. Natalma was sent to the veterinary clinic at the University of Pennsylvania to have the chip surgically removed and then was returned to Canada to recuperate.

The following spring Natalma was shipped to Lexington, Kentucky to join Victoria Park, Windfields first Kentucky Derby candidate. Like Nearctic, Victoria Park had begun his racing life in the care of Pete McCann. Victoria Park was ridden in the mornings by Pete McCann, and in the races by Bennie Sorensen. Victoria Park had blistering speed (and he was slightly pigeon-toed.) He won his first four races. Then Joe Thomas fired Bennie Sorensen and hired one "R. Guilierrez" to ride Victoria Park in his next race. Victoria Park fell on his nose coming out of the starting gate and tore a chunk of flesh from his heel when he scrambled to get back on his feet. The horse was sidelined; Guilierrez was never mentioned again; but Victoria Park was sent to Luro, who raced him twice, unsuccessfully in U.S. races. Thomas then brought Victoria Park back to Canada. However, Luro, not Pete McCann was listed thereafter as his trainer.

Luro had never trained a Kentucky Derby horse but tended not to think small. Soon he had himself convinced that between them, Natalma and Victoria Park were going to win both the Kentucky

Oaks and the Kentucky Derby. Or so he told the assembled reporters.

Opening day of the spring meet at Keeneland, Natalma was entered in a minor event, her first race of the year. She finished out of the money. A week later, however, Natalma came blasting off the pace and won the fifth race of the day by a length and three-quarters. It was a curious performance: lacklustre one week, brilliant the next. Shades of Eugenia II, Luro's filly that ran a dismal race one afternoon but several days later won the Canadian International Championship and considerable money for her backers in what was referred to in Joe Hirsch's biography of Luro, as the "Canadian Caper."

The following day Natalma was scratched from the Kentucky Oaks "because of a chipped bone in her left knee." It was the end of Natalma's brief racing career. She stayed in Kentucky with Victoria Park, however, travelling with him to Baltimore for the Preakness Stakes and to Canada for the Queen's Plate. Instead of getting off the van at Woodbine racetrack, however, Natalma was driven to the National Stud Farm. Taylor had determined that she was to be retired and bred to one of his stallions.

Gil Darlington, manager of the National Stud, decided that of all the Taylor horses, Nearctic was the best match: they were both young. Natalma was very well-bred; and Canadian horse breeders were not exactly lining up to have their mares mated with Nearctic.

"I can remember the trouble I had selling services to Nearctic for $2,500 each," recalled Darlington years later. "Canadian breeders simply will not patronize an unproven horse, so you have to make him yourself, as we did…"

This historic mating would, of course, bring us Northern Dancer.

Northern Dancer bore scant resemblance to his sire. Instead he resembled his maternal grandsire's branch of the family. The small, but mighty matriarch, Selene, dam of Hyperion, granddam of Nearctic is also in the family of Natalma. Selene's son, Sickle, is the great-grandsire of Natalma's sire, Native Dancer.

Where Nearctic was a free-running horse, Northern Dancer

galloped with a short choppy stride. Northern Dancer was propelled by a huge heart and even huger hind quarters, perhaps an inheritance from those stout Scottish Galloway running horses that provided the foundation stock for the Thoroughbred all those centuries ago.

Northern Dancer's racing life bore a resemblance to that of his sire, Nearctic—especially the bungling. He began his training with Pete McCann, but before he started racing he was sent to the Canadian shedrow of Horatio Luro. (Luro himself was not in Canada; rather, he was gallivanting between Belmont Park, France and California.)

Why send Northern Dancer to Luro? According to Joe Thomas: "It seemed logical to send him to Luro, as he'd trained the dam and had had such bad luck with her." One would be hard-pressed to find a more illogical explanation. Natalma broke down twice while under the care of Luro—a curious reason to send another horse to him. Victoria Park eventually went lame with Luro, as would Northern Dancer.

Luro sent his most recent assistant, Thomas (Peaches) Flemming to Toronto to maintain his Canadian division. Mid-July 1963, Taylor, accompanied by Thomas, visited the track to check on his horses. During the tour they stopped by Northern Dancer's stall. Taylor asked Flemming when Northern Dancer would be starting in a race. The colt had been held back because he had suffered cracked heels, a form of psoriasis, which can take considerable time and care to clear up.

Thomas then turned to Flemming and told him it was time to start Northern Dancer. Flemming was reluctant. According to Thomas: "He told me that he thought Northern Dancer was still too green, but I said, 'Oh hell, go ahead and run him.'"

Like Nearctic, Northern Dancer had a long list of different jockeys. His first was Ron Turcotte, a young apprentice from New Brunswick, who was introduced to Thoroughbreds and encouraged to be a rider by Pete McCann. Conversely Luro fired him. Ron

Turcotte would go on to become one of the greatest jockeys of all time riding Secretariat's in his stunning 1973 U.S. Triple Crown triumph.

When Northern Dancer became a Kentucky Derby candidate, the fact that he arrived in Louisville in one piece is more astonishing than his blistering two-minute victory in the Derby.

On the morning prior to the Florida Derby, his final prep race before travelling to Kentucky, Ramón Hernandez, Northern Dancer's regular exercise rider was in Toronto, so the horse was ridden by a substitute. (Why Hernandez would travel to Toronto during the first week of April, the day before his mount was in the Florida Derby, has never been answered.)

Northern Dancer was not an easy horse to ride. Everyone knew that he was volatile and headstrong. Whatever happened that fateful morning, Northern Dancer got the bit in his teeth, took off, and tore around the training track. With his substitute rider hauling on his reins, Northern Dancer covered five furlongs in a blistering 58.6 seconds. The horse had run his race, a day early. It seemed inconceivable that he would have the reserves to run the equivalent of back-to-back races, but he did. And he won. Few knew of the previous day's "race," so most were unimpressed with his form, including his rider that day, Bill Shoemaker, who opted to ride Hill Rise in the forthcoming Kentucky Derby.

When Northern Dancer arrived in Kentucky to prepare for the big race, he still did not have a rider. Finally Luro decided on jockey Bill Hartack, but Joe Thomas disagreed, and was so quoted in the Toronto media.

Luro was not pleased. "I am running the stable!" he fumed in the next edition.

Oblivious to the bickering, Northern Dancer won the Kentucky Derby in record time. No sooner had he won the Preakness, the second race of the U.S. Triple Crown, than he was again at the centre of discord.

At the party at Pimlico's Members Club to celebrate Northern Dancer's victory, the assembled crowd were taken aback when Luro confided that Northern Dancer had "distance limitations," and would not be running him in the third U.S. Triple Crown race, the Belmont Stakes. But, no one was more surprised at the announcement that Northern Dancer's owner, E.P. Taylor, who overruled Luro the following morning. Northern Dancer ran in the Belmont Stakes.

However, Luro was not alone in his opinion that Northern Dancer had distance limitations. Hartack did not think that Northern Dancer was up to the Belmont's mile-and-a-half, and rode him accordingly. The pace was exceedingly slow. For most of the race Hartack had such a strong hold on Northern Dancer that the colt was fairly levitating off the ground with each constricted stride. Northern Dancer fought and fought his rider. By the time Hartack released his stranglehold, Northern Dancer had used up his reserves. So much dirt was thrown up from the heels of the horses in front of him, that for two hours following the race Northern Dancer coughed up dirt. Still, the colt managed a valiant third—at the price of a bowed tendon.

Northern Dancer did race one more time, in the Queen's Plate, which he won on sheer heart, and three legs. The tendon was, by now, fairly swollen. Northern Dancer's racing days were over.

Northern Dancer stood his first year at stud in 1965. His fee was $10,000 for a live foal. By 1984, his fee was $500,000, no guarantee. Thereafter until Northern Dancer retired from stud on 15 April 1987, as much as $1 million was paid for a single breeding with no guarantee.

The main reason behind these extraordinary prices was the horse called Nijinsky. This son of Flaming Page and Northern Dancer was foaled in 1967; purchased as a yearling by American Charles Engelhard; and sent to Ireland to train with Vincent O'Brien. In 1970 Nijinsky won the British Triple Crown—the Guineas, the Derby, and the St. Leger—the first horse to do so since Bahram, in

1935. No horse has duplicated the feat since Nijinsky. It is unlikely one ever will. Nijinsky was brilliant, beautiful, and looked nothing like his sire. Instead, Nijinsky resembled his grandsire, Nearctic. Still, few knew much about Nearctic. His story, particularly what he had endured, already had vaporized, and all that was left behind were some of the statistics—none of the reality.

So, initially, it was thought that Nijinsky was a fluke. Seven years later, The Minstrel, another son of Northern Dancer, won the Derby, and this one looked like his sire. Taylor syndicated the colt for a whooping $9 million; and Northern Dancer and many of his offsprings became more valuable than gold.

"Heredity sometimes works in inscrutable ways. In the Deauville paddock before the Prix Morny, Nonoalco was reminiscent of Nijinsky by his bright bay colour, his bearing, his commanding presence, and physique and length of leg. But the most striking physical characteristic of their close common ancestor, Nearctic, who is almost black, is the extraordinary length which makes him resemble one of those expansible dining room tables in which a leaf has been inserted to accommodate the influx of guests."

PETER WILLETT, *HORSE AND HOUND*

Foaled in 1971, Nonoalco, the handsome son of Nearctic and the mare Seximee, was a brilliant racehorse. Bred in North America, Nonoalco was purchased as a yearling at the Keeneland July Yearling Sale by the Mexican film actress, Maria-Felix Berger. She paid $30,000 for the colt and shipped him to France where he would train under the tutelage of François Boutin.

Nonoalco developed into a big grand-looking colt, and appeared far more mature than any of the other two-year-olds of his generation in France. At the end of his first racing season, Nonoalco was weighted just behind Mississippian on the 1973 French Handicap Optional.

In the Prix Yacowlef, Boutin hired the successful young jockey

Philippe Pacquet to ride Nonoalco. For some reason Pacquet deemed it necessary to go to the whip—twice. Each time Nonoalco felt the sting, he shot forward, by at least four lengths. Nonoalco won the race by eight lengths and broke the record set by the great racemare, Dahlia, the previous year.

Boutin commissioned veteran jockey, Lester Piggott to ride Nonoalco in his next race, the Prix Morny, and Pacquet watched from the sidelines as Piggott sat perfectly still in the saddle and allowed Nonoalco to run his own race. Nonoalco coasted effortlessly across the finish three lengths ahead of his nearest rivals. It was Nonoalco's second record-breaking victory in a fortnight and the crowd hurried to the winner's enclosure to see this exceptional colt and the celebrities that surrounded him.

When Nonoalco's owner, Maria-Felix Berger, reached the enclosure, the exuberant actress planted a kiss on the cheek of the usually sombre-looking Piggott; a huge grin unfurled across the leathery features of the champion jockey. Nonoalco appeared calm and unperturbed by all the excitement.

"Everybody had something to say, but perhaps the most significant remark was Piggott's own admission that the colt was the fastest two-year-old he had ever ridden," said Peter Willett in the *Horse and Hound.*

In the Grand Criterium, the soft, deep turf proved Nonoalco's undoing. In the straight, Nonoalco galloped into the lead, but soon Mississippian had drawn up alongside and the two colts matched each other, stride for stride, to the finish. Nonoalco, who generally had blistering acceleration, appeared to struggle with the soft going, while Mississippian seemed untroubled by the condition of the course. At the wire Mississippian won by a nose from Nonoalco.

The following year Nonoalco was sent to England and won the Two Thousand Guineas by one-and-a-half lengths over a good field that included Giacometti, Apalachee and Northern Taste. Back in France, Nonoalco also won the Prix Jacques le Marois, Prix Rond-

Point and Prix Montencia, but in the English Derby at Epsom, Nonoalco, wrote John Aiscan, "found the distance beyond him."

Nonoalco's final race was the Prix du Moulin de Longchamp. The ground was soft and deep, and this star of the French turf crossed the finish at the back of the pack. Nonoalco had pulled a muscle and was retired to the French stud, Haras de Meautry, where in 1975 Nonoalco would begin covering mares. In 1981, Nonoalco was sent to Japan.

His influence on Japanese Thoroughbreds is extensive, but he is perhaps most celebrated as the sire of Katies, dam of the great champion and national equine heroine, Hishi Amazon. Another Nonoalco daughter, Cargo, is the dam of 2000 Preakness winner, Red Bullet, and Millennium Allstar, a handsome chestnut stakes winner in Canada.

A Nonoalco grandson, Reprimand, stands at Fawley Stud in Oxfordshire, England. At 16.2 hands high, Reprimand has a good shoulder, well-set neck and sturdy quarters. Like his great-grandsire, Nearctic, Reprimand's two hind legs are capped with short white socks. Reprimand raced in Great Britain (and once in Italy) during the late 1980s. Unbeaten at two, Reprimand raced to four and was never unplaced. He was a leading sire in 1998, with 25 winners of 32 races.

Icecapade, like Northern Dancer, is the son of a Native Dancer daughter. His dam, Shenanigans, was also dam of Ruffian. During two brief seasons, 1974 and 1975, Ruffian was proclaimed the greatest filly in U.S. Thoroughbred sport. She was grand-looking, a dark, dark, bay—almost black—with a small diamond-shaped star on the centre of her forehead. Unbeaten in ten races, she shattered one track record after another. Fans were enraptured by her sheer beauty, her awesome spirit and her blistering speed.

The dream died, however, on 6 July 1975 during a mile-and-a-quarter match race at Belmont Park between Ruffian and Kentucky Derby winner Foolish Pleasure. (The promoters called it "the battle of the sexes.") Close to twenty million North Americans were watching their televisions sets when Ruffian, out in front, broke down. That evening Ruffian was euthanized.

Ruffian's half-brother, Icecapade, did not possess the brilliance of Ruffian—few do—but was sound and consistent. Like Native Dancer, Icecapade was a grey. While not as big as Native Dancer, Icecapade was a well proportioned horse, with sturdy limbs.

Icecapade raced as a two-, three-and-four-year-old. He won thirteen races, including the Sarnac Stakes, Kelso Handicap, Longport Handicap and Stuyvesant Handicap.

Icecapade's son, Wild Again, was the winner of the 1984 Breeders' Cup Classic. In 1997, Elmhurst, a son of Wild Again, won the Breeders' Cup Sprint, making Elmhurst and Wild Again the fourth father-son pair of Breeders' Cup winners.

That same year, Favorite Trick won the Breeders' Cup Juvenile and was named Horse of the Year in the United States. A great-grandson of Icecapade, Favorite Trick is by Phone Trick, by Clever Trick. A huge and solid horse, Phone Trick stood at Walmac International in Kentucky, but was sold in 2001 to stand in New York.

Besides Elmhurst, nineteen-year-old Wild Again has sired approximately sixty stakes winners, including Wilderness Song, whose accomplishments include the top U.S. distaff race, the Grade I Spinster Stakes. Wilderness Song won $1.5 million in purse money, and the Sovereign Award as Champion Older Mare in Canada. Wild Again is also the sire of Whiskey Wisdom, who stands at Windfields Farm. Like Nearctic, Whiskey Wisdom is a very dark bay, almost black, colt; he is, however, of a more peaceful disposition.

Following in his sire's footsteps, Whiskey Wisdom ran in the Breeders' Cup Classic, in 1997. He finished a hard-running third, but due to a rider error on the part of Pat Day he was moved from third to fourth. These days, Whiskey Wisdom has a number of very fine-looking foals grazing and frolicking about Windfields Farm paddocks, and members of his first crop of two-year-olds are at the track winning races.

Another of Nearctic's sons to establish a significant sire line was Explodent. A stakes winner of eight races, Explodent has sired over sixty stakes winners, including Bex, the Champion three-year-old filly in Ireland, and multiple Grade I winners in the United States, Mi Selecto and Exchange.

Another Explodent son is Explosive Red. He was started eleven times at two: he won the Cup and Saucer Stakes, 1-1/16 miles over the turf at Woodbine, and was second in the Summer Stakes G-3. At three, Explosive Red was the front-running winner of the Grade I Hollywood Derby, defeating Cigar and the Irish horse, Fastness, at equal weights. He won the American Derby G-2, and the Forerunner Stakes G-3.

He raced once at four, finishing second behind the very excellent turf horse, Bien Bien, in the Grade II in the San Marcos Handicap, 1-1/16 over the turf. His owners brought him back to race in his five-year-old year, starting him twice, but to no avail. Explosive Red now stands at stud in Florida.

Next to Northern Dancer, my favourite Nearctic son was Briartic. Like his sire, Briartic was raced excessively and passed around among at least three trainers; yet he raced through to his six-year-old season. He was started sixty-three times; thirteen as a two-year-old. His racing debut was a 5-1/2 furlong maiden race at Woodbine. Like Nearctic, he bolted out of the gate, took command and led all the way, to win by 3-1/4 lengths over a very good field including Kennedy Road and Lord Vancouver.

A week later he was back in the starting gate for the Victoria Stakes. Again, Briartic was first out of the gate and grabbed the lead. By halfway, Kennedy Road had drawn up alongside, but Briartic dug in and was first across the finish, several lengths ahead of Kennedy Road. Later that summer, Briartic was shipped to Bluebonnets in Montreal to contest the Fleur de Lys Stakes. It is unclear exactly what happened, but Briartic was fractious in the starting gate, and the track was a sea of mud. Slow out of the gate, Briartic finished a distant sixth.

After Bluebonnets, Briartic never again seemed the same horse. He was beaten by a neck by Kennedy Road in a prep for the Coronation Futurity, one of Canada's top two-year-old races. A week later, in the Futurity itself, he ran unplaced. In Canada's other top juvenile race, the Cup and Saucer Stakes, Briartic finished third behind Kennedy Road. He was however, in the frame in several other stakes races.

Briartic was sent to the post sixteen times at three. He won the Marine Stakes by two lengths over Kennedy Road and won a number of allowance races in Canada and the United States. He was third in the Queen's Plate Trials, but was unplaced in the Queen's Plate.

At two, Briartic had been handled by Canadian conditioner, J. Mort Hardy, but for the following season was sent to another Canadian, A.G "Andy" Smithers. At four Briartic won four stakes races, from six to nine furlongs and he ran second to Kennedy Road in the Dominion Day Handicap at Woodbine. He was then shipped across the continent to Seattle, where he was beaten by a nose in the Longacres Mile Handicap.

At five Briartic began racing in Florida, where he won two allowance races, after which he was shipped to California—and a new trainer—T.W. Dunn. Briartic went on to win a mile allowance, the seven-furlong Lakes and Flowers Handicap, two mile-and-a-sixteenth allowance races, and placed second in the Leland Bay Handicap at California's Bay Meadows.

Briartic won his first start at six at Santa Anita; he was raced twice more, but was unplaced and retired to stud. Briartic stood his first season in 1974 at the Sarnia, Ontario farm of Dr. M.F. Bennett, part owner and breeder of the horse. Later that year Windfields arranged to syndicate Briartic and to stand him at Windfields [formerly National Stud] farm in Oshawa, Ontario beginning in the 1975 breeding season.

Briartic was a very dark chestnut. His sole white marking was a small star beneath his forelock. He stood 16 hands, but looked bigger, probably because, like Nearctic, he was so long in the back, had an awesome shoulder and powerful hindquarters.

Briartic shows his Nearctic lineage in stamina and longevity. Nearctic was started forty-seven times; Briartic, an excessive sixty-three times. Briartic also exemplifies that group of Nearctic's offspring that were overlooked, or perhaps obscured by the brilliance of Nearctic's foremost son, Northern Dancer. Briartic did not breed great numbers of mares, merely fifteen in his first year at stud. Still, all fifteen mares gave birth to healthy foals, and all of whom raced.

From this small crop came the Graded stakes-winning filly,

Impetuous Gal. Briartic's second crop included Canada's champion three-year-old of 1979, Steady Growth. In Canada, Steady Growth's stakes laurels included the Queen's Plate; and, in the United States, the Grade II Arlington Classic. In 1982 Briartic had his second Queen's Plate winner, Son of Briartic.

Briartic died in 1994.

APPENDICES

Approximately seventy-five per cent of Thoroughbreds foaled in the spring of 2001 have Nearctic in their bloodlines. There are many reasons behind this, not the least of which was the pursuit of Northern Dancer yearling colts in the 1980s. The following lists attempt to offer some idea of the extent of Nearctic's influence through his most prominent sons. The list is by no means complete, nor does it include the many exceptional horses that descend maternally.

Some of these notable stallions, out of great-granddaughters, include: Dubai Millennium - dam Angel Fever, by Danzig, by Northern Dancer; Fusaichi Pegasus - dam Colorado Dancer, by Shareef Dancer, by Northern Dancer; With Approval - dam Passing Mood, out of Cool Mood, by Northern Dancer. The dam of Swain, Love Smitten, is a granddaughter. Mark of Esteem, son of Homage (by Ajdal), is a great-great grandson. And on and on and on.

BRIARTIC

(Sweet Lady Briar — Round Table) 1968

Son of Briartic (USA)

Arctic Twister

Arctic Blitz

Briartic Command

Steady Growth

Steady Effort

Hasty Growth

EXPLODENT

(Venomous — Mel Hash) 1969

Commitisize

Exbourne

Expelled (USA)

Explosive Bid (USA)

Bidding Proud

Explosive Red (USA)

Mi Selecto

ICECAPADE

(Shenanigans — Native Dancer) 1969

Clever Trick (USA)

Anet (USA)

Cold Reality

Phone Trick (USA)

Caller I.D. (USA)

Favorite Trick (USA)

Phone Saga

Tricky Creek (USA)

Tricky Fun (USA)

Wild Again (USA)

Nines Wild

Whiskey Wisdom (Can)

Wild Event (USA)

Wild Gambler (USA)

Wild Gold (USA)

Wild Rush (USA)

Wild Syn (USA)

Wild Zone (USA)

NONOALCO

(Seximee — Hasty Road) 1971

Nikos (Fr)

Dai Yusaku (Jpn)

Kashima Wing (Jpn)

NORTHERN DANCER

(Natalma — Native Dancer) 1961

Ajdal

Alwasmi (Ger)

Be My Guest (Ire)

Anfield (Jpn)

Turfkonig (Ger)

Assert (Ire)

Dancehall (Jpn)

Double Bed (Fr)

Go and Go

Pelder (GB)

Pentire (Jpn)

Raami (Aus)

Carnivalay (USA)

Amerivaly (USA)

Compliance

Fourstars Allstar (Ire)

Dance Spell

Dancing Count

Danzatore (USA)

Danzig (USA)

    Allied Flag (SAf)

        Classic Flag (SAf)

    Alfaari

        Always Fair

    Anabaa (Fr/Aus)

    Ascot Knight (Can)

    Belong to Me (USA)

        Lucky Roberto (USA)

    Bianconi (USA)

    Boundary (USA)

    Chief's Crown

        Azzaam (Aus)

        Bonus Money

        Chief Bearheart (Jpn)

        Erhaab (GB)

        Grand Lodge (Ire/Aus)

    Danehill (Ire/Aus)

        Commands (Aus)

        Danasinga

        Danehill Dancer (Ire)

        Danewin

        Danzero (Aus)

        Desert King (Ire/Aus)

        Flying Spur (Aus)

        Nothin Leica (Aus)

        Redoute's Choice (Aus)

        Shovhog (Aus)

        Tiger Hill (Fr)

    Dayjur (USA)

    Deerhound (USA)

    Dove Hunt

    Dumaani (USA)

    Foxhound (Ire/Chi)

    Furiously

        Game Plan

    Green Desert (GB)

        Desert Sun (GB)

        Desert Style (Ire)

        Owington (GB)

        Volksraad (NZ)

    Hamas (Ire)

    Honor Grades (USA)

    Katowice (USA)

    Langfuhr (USA/Aus)

    Lure (USA)

    Maroof (NZ)

    Military (USA)

    Mister C (Aus)

    National Assembly (SAf)

        National Emblem (SAf)

    Nicholas

    Partner's Hero (USA)

    Perugino (Ire/Aus)

    Pine Bluff (USA)

        Lil's Lad (USA)

    Polish Navy (USA)

        Ghazi

        Sea Hero (Tur)

    Polish Numbers (USA)

    Polish Precedent (GB)

        Pilsudski (Ire/Jpn)

    Roi Danzig (Ity)

    Strolling Along (USA)

    Zieten (Fr)

NORTHERN DANCER

Danzig (continued)

Ziggy's Boy

Blitzer

Zignew

Dixieland Band (USA)

Chimes Band (USA)

Citidancer (USA)

Dixie Brass (USA)

Dixieland Brass (Can)

Jambalaya Jazz (USA)

Placid Fund

Southern Rythm

El Gran Senor

Belmez (Fr)

Lit de Justice (USA)

Helmsman (USA)

Rodrigo de Triano (Jpn)

Saratoga Springs (Fr/Aus)

Vincent Russell

Eskimo (USA)

Fabulous Dancer (Fr)

Fairy King

Bartok (Ire/USA)

Helissio (Jpn)

Makbul (GB)

Revoque (Ire)

Second Empire (Ire)

Turtle Island (Ire)

Island Sands

Far North

The Wicked North (USA)

Fire Dancer

Grand Chaudiere

Hero's Honor (Fr)

Jugah (Aus)

Local Talent (USA)

Larry The Legend (USA)

Lomond (Ity)

Valanour (Fr)

Rokeby

Steerforth

Lyphard

Al Nasr (Ger)

Alzao (Ire)

Waky Nao (Ger)

Shafouri

Bellypha (Jpn)

Mendez (Jpn)

Linamix (Fr)

Dahar

Buckhar

Dancing Brave

Commander in Chief (Jpn)

White Muzzle (Jpn)

Dreams To Reality (Fr)

Elliodor (SAf)

Model Man (SAf)

Special Preview (SAf)

Falstaff

Apollo

Ghadeer (Brz)

Falcon Jet (Brz)

Manilla (Tur)

Bien Bien (GB)

NORTHERN DANCER

Nijinsky (continued)

    Sky Classic (USA)

    Sportin' Life

        Bet Twice

    Sword Dance (USA)

        Marlin (USA)

    Tights (NZ)

    Western Symphony (Aus)

        Procol Harum

    Whiskey Road

        Strawberry Road (Aus)

          Mud Route (USA)

    Yeats (Aus)

        Our Poetic Prince (Aus)

Northern Answer

    Greek Answer

Northern Baby (USA)

    Deposit Ticket (USA)

    Kreisler (NZ)

Northern Bay

Northern Jove

    Equalize (Arg)

        Munecote (Arg)

Northern Taste (Jpn)

    Amber Shadai (Jpn)

        Mejiro Ryan (Jpn)

Northfields

    Pass No Sale (Jpn)

    Northjet (Ger)

Nureyev (USA)

    Alwuhush (Ger)

    Atticus (USA)

Fadeyev (Arg)

Fasliyev (Ire)

Fotitieng (Jpn)

Goldneyev (Fr)

    Gold Away (Fr)

Joyeux Danseur (USA)

Lead On Time (Ger)

    Fraam (GB)

Peintre Celebre (Ire/Aus)

Polar Falcon (GB)

    Pivotal (GB)

Robin des Bois (Arg)

    Gentlemen (USA)

Robin des Pins

Rudimentary (GB)

Soviet Star (Ire)

    Ashkalani (Aus/Ire)

Spinning World (USA/NZ)

Theatrical (USA)

    Geri (Jpn)

    Royal Anthem (USA)

Zilzal (GB)

    Among Men (Ire)

One For All

Rakeen (SAf)

    Jet Master (SAf)

Razeen (USA)

Sadler's Wells (Ire)

    Barathea (Ire)

    Carnegie (Jpn)

    Desert Secret (Ire)

    Dream Well (Jpn)

    Dushyantor (Ire)

El Prado (USA)

Entrepreneur (Ire/Aus)

Fort Wood (SAf)

    Horse Chestnut (USA)

In The Wings (Ire)

    Singspiel (GB)

    Winged Love

King of Kings (USA/Aus)

King's Theatre (Ire/Aus)

Opera House (Jpn)

Saddlers' Hall (Ire)

    Silver Patriarch (Ire)

Scenic (Aus)

    Blevic (Aus)

Stagecoach (Chi)

Walter Willy

Secreto (Jpn)

Shareef Dancer

    Rock Hopper (Ire)

    Nediym (Aus)

        General Nediym (Aus)

Somethingfabulous

    Fabulous Champ (USA)

    Something Lucky (USA)

Sovereign Dancer

    Dins Dancer (USA)

    Gate Dancer

    Leo Castelli (USA)

    Louis Quatorze (USA/Aus)

    Priolo (Ire)

        Sendawar (Fr)

    Reign Road

    Wall Street Dancer

Staff Writer

Storm Bird

    Bluebird (Ire)

        Blues Traveller (Ire)

        Dolphin Street (Ire)

        Lake Coniston (Ire)

    Mujadil (Ire)

    Mukaddamah (Ire)

    Personal Hope (SAf)

    Storm Cat (USA)

        Aljabr (USA)

        Catrail (USA)

        Delineator (USA)

        Exploit (USA)

        Forest Wildcat (USA)

        Forestry (USA)

        Future Storm (USA)

        Hennessy (Jpn/Aus)

        Sir Cat (USA)

        Storm Creek (USA)

        Stormin Fever (USA)

        Tabasco Cat (USA)

    Summer Squall (USA)

        Charismatic (USA)

The Minstrel

    L'Emigrant

    Palace Music (Aus)

        Naturalism (Aus)

Thorn Dance (USA)

    General Monash (Ire)

Topsider

    Assatis (Jpn)

NORTHERN DANCER (continued)

Try My Best

    Last Tycoon (Jpn)

        Bigstone (China)

        Ezzoud (GB)

        Knowledge (Aus)

        Lost World (Ity)

        Monde Bleu (Aus)

    Waajib

        Royal Applause (GB)

Unfuwain (GB)

    Alhaarth (Ire)

Viceregal

    Esclavo

    Solarstern

Vice Regent

    Archregent (Aus)

    Deputy Minister (USA)

        Awesome Again (USA)

        Always A Classic (Tur)

        Dehere (Jpn/Aus)

        Defrere (USA)

        Deputy Commander (USA)

        Earth Star

        Flag Down (USA/Aus)

        French Deputy (USA)

        Mane Minister (Brz)

        Open Forum (USA)

        Salt Lake (USA/Aus)

            Ordway (USA)

        Silver Deputy (USA)

            Archers Bay (Can)

            Statesmanship (USA)

    Touch Gold (USA)

    Iskandar Elakbar (Can)

    New Regent (Aus)

    Regal Classic (USA/Aus)

    Regal Embrace

    Regal Intention (Can)

FAMILY TREE

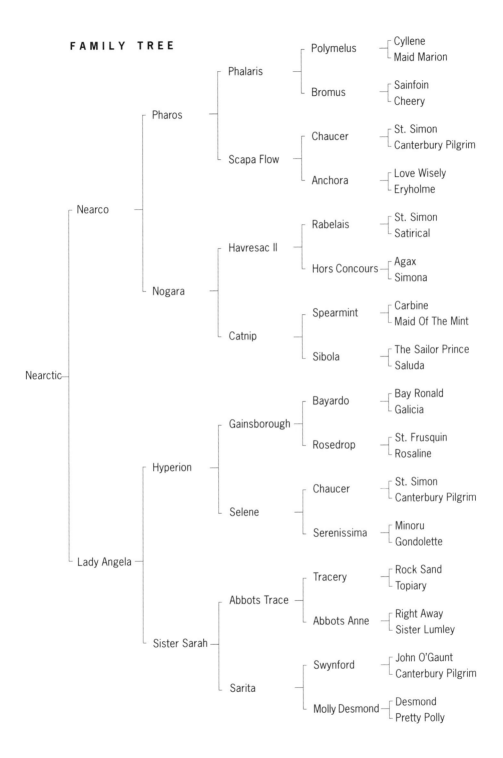

Nearctic
├─ Nearco
│ ├─ Pharos
│ │ ├─ Phalaris
│ │ │ ├─ Polymelus
│ │ │ │ ├─ Cyllene
│ │ │ │ └─ Maid Marion
│ │ │ └─ Bromus
│ │ │   ├─ Sainfoin
│ │ │   └─ Cheery
│ │ └─ Scapa Flow
│ │   ├─ Chaucer
│ │   │ ├─ St. Simon
│ │   │ └─ Canterbury Pilgrim
│ │   └─ Anchora
│ │   ├─ Love Wisely
│ │   └─ Eryholme
│ └─ Nogara
│   ├─ Havresac II
│   │ ├─ Rabelais
│   │ │ ├─ St. Simon
│   │ │ └─ Satirical
│   │ └─ Hors Concours
│   │   ├─ Agax
│   │   └─ Simona
│   └─ Catnip
│   ├─ Spearmint
│   │ ├─ Carbine
│   │ └─ Maid Of The Mint
│   └─ Sibola
│   ├─ The Sailor Prince
│   └─ Saluda
└─ Lady Angela
   ├─ Hyperion
   │ ├─ Gainsborough
   │ │ ├─ Bayardo
   │ │ │ ├─ Bay Ronald
   │ │ │ └─ Galicia
   │ │ └─ Rosedrop
   │ │   ├─ St. Frusquin
   │ │   └─ Rosaline
   │ └─ Selene
   │   ├─ Chaucer
   │   │ ├─ St. Simon
   │   │ └─ Canterbury Pilgrim
   │   └─ Serenissima
   │   ├─ Minoru
   │   └─ Gondolette
   └─ Sister Sarah
      ├─ Abbots Trace
      │ ├─ Tracery
      │ │ ├─ Rock Sand
      │ │ └─ Topiary
      │ └─ Abbots Anne
      │   ├─ Right Away
      │   └─ Sister Lumley
      └─ Sarita
         ├─ Swynford
         │ ├─ John O'Gaunt
         │ └─ Canterbury Pilgrim
         └─ Molly Desmond
            ├─ Desmond
            └─ Pretty Polly

della Rochetta, Mario Incisa. *The Tesios As I Knew Them*. London: J.A. Allen, 1979

Graham, Clive. *Hyperion*. London: J.A. Allen, 1967

Herbert, Ivor (advisory editor). *Horse Racing: The Complete Guide to the World of the Turf*. London: William Collins & Son, 1980

Hirsch, Joe. *The Grand Senor: The Fabulous Career of Horatio Luro*. Lexington: The Blood-Horse, 1989

Hislop, John and Swannell, Dave. *The Faber Book of the Turf*. London: Faber and Faber, 1990

Longrigg, Roger. *The History of Horse Racing*. New York: Stein & Day, 1972

Morris, Tony. *Thoroughbred Stallions*. Swindon: The Crowood Press, 1970

Robertson, William H.P. *The History of Thoroughbred Racing in North America*. Englewood Cliffs, N.J. Prentice Hall, 1964

Tesio, Federico. *Breeding The Racehorse*. London: J.A. Allen, 1958

Varola, Franco. *The Tesio Myth*. London: J.A. Allen, 1984

NEWSPAPERS AND MAGAZINES

The Daily Racing Form, Horse and Hound, Canadian Horse, Thoroughbred Times, The Blood-Horse, The Toronto Star, Toronto Telegram.

PHOTO CREDITS

Racing photos through to 1958: Turofsky; 1959: Michael Burns. All other photos courtesy of Windfields Farm.

ACKNOWLEDGEMENTS

ACKNOWLEDGEMENTS

Authors, like race horses, are dependent upon a team of professionals to get them across the finish line. The fortunate writers end up like Nijinsky, surrounded by the very best people. I am one of the fortunate writers.

Entering the homestretch, the most important person, for me, at least, is the editor. Charis Wahl may not be the world's greatest handicapper, but she one of its shrewdest editors. She is also thoughtful, cheerful and has a canny sense of humour—a great bonus in those final few furlongs.

Right from our first meeting at a local coffee shop, the book's designer, Saskia Rowley, has had an almost uncanny sense of this book. She created the jacket cover, long before I'd finished writing it. Saskia's commitment to the project is evident throughout.

Dark Horse was a challenging book, both to research and to write, so I am very grateful to all the people who lent their support and expertise. My special thanks go to Beth Heriot for her ongoing encouragement; Bill Reeves for sharing his recollections; Reta Irwin-McCann for somehow getting her father to the family reunion; Michael Magee for his insights.

And thanks to Scott Brown, Bob Careless, Paul Dillon, Meg Floyd, Elizabeth Irons, Lorraine O'Brien, Toru Shirai, Bill Talon, and Edward Taylor. Gratitude to my fitness experts, Peggy Buchar and Richard Lacroix for keeping me going; and to Cathy Schenck and Phyllis Rogers for maintaining the marvelous Keeneland library. Thank you to Kunio Serizawa, editor-in-chief of *Gallop*, for inviting me to write for his magazine, which led me to start questioning why so little was known of Nearctic. And to Jiro O'hara for all those years of translations. And I am indebted to Gail Hamilton and Janet Todd for reading the manuscript in its many incarnations.

But of all the people in my life, I am particularly grateful to Judith Mappin, my partner in Val d'Argent—both the horse and I have benefitted enormously from her patience and her wisdom.

Years ago Judy and I rode together at Windfields and often talked about getting a Thoroughbred or two. But since she and her family live in Montreal and I am in Toronto, we never seemed get much past talking and attending the occasional yearling sale. Then, along came Val d'Argent. It took a long time just to win his trust. Many would have given up on him and invested in a horse more malleable. Where I worried that we were not getting anywhere with him, Judy continued to be unperturbed by our almost infinitesimal progress. Eventually, I guess, her wisdom began to penetrate. I stopped worrying. Val d'Argent stopped going ballistic.

And, of course, if it were not for Val d'Argent, I wonder if I would have tackled *Dark Horse*. So I am grateful to Val, not only for pushing me to learn more about his great-great-grandsire, but for all he has taught me.

Finally I must pay tribute to all the gallant Thoroughbreds, the noblest creatures on earth. They give all they have and ask for so little in return. We have so much to learn from them.

VAL D'ARGENT AND FRIENDS